WHITEWATER COOKS

with passion

ISBN 978-0-9811424-2-5

Author: Shelley Adams **whitewatercooks.com**
Photography: David R. Gluns **gluns.ca**
Design and layout: Dale Nigel Goble **dngstudio.com**

Published by Alicon Holdings Ltd., Nelson BC
Printed and bound in Canada by Friesens Book Division

Thanks to the owners of Whitewater Ski Resort: Dean Prodan, Mitch Putnam, Andrew Kyle.

I thank our recipe contributors with all my heart
Pat McLaughlin, Ali Adams,Gail Morrison, Margie Rosling, Barb Gosney, Sheri Weichel, Clare Hetherington, Tana Tocher, Emmy Mcknight, Marianne Abraham, Jan Sorensen, Amanda Skidmore, Laura Carter, Kim Irving, Annie Bailey, Andrea Manson, Michele Repine, Linda Klein, Liz Abraham,Jeff Bruce, Petra Lehmann, Yoshi Shirotani, Brent Petkau, Laurel Colins, Nancy Selwood

Distributed by Sandhill Book Marketing **sandhillbooks.com** **info@sandhillbooks.com**
Distributed by Partners Publishing Group **partnerspublishinggroup.com** **info@partnerspublishinggroup.com**

To order all books in the Whitewater Cooks series visit skiwhitewater.com

bringing people together...

There are so many things that have inspired me to create Whitewater Cooks with Passion. It's my passion to experiment with the flavours, textures, and colours of carefully selected ingredients in order to create easy and delicious meals that are works of art for both the eyes and the palate. The inspiration also comes from my passion for sharing these creations with others - so that they too will bring people together at their tables to experience the healthy richness of fresh food that is beautifully prepared.

Whether joining my husband at day's end for a glass of wine and a plate of Braised Fresh Artichokes, being together with my grown children sharing Seared Scallop and Crispy Prosciutto Salad, or gathering with friends to dine on Grilled Beef with Chimichurri Sauce, the creation and presentation of simple and innovative recipes brings me great happiness. I hope you will find the same pleasure with these recipes and the many more that are included in this book.

I want these recipes to bring people together. It's a time to relax, converse, laugh, discuss topics great and small while enjoying the delicious, yet easy to prepare recipes thoughtfully compiled in my new book. In the spirit of the great Julia Child, with whom I share a passion for cooking:

"Bon Appétit!" – from my table to yours.

Shelley

acknowledgements

Creating a cookbook involves many people through the various stages from idea to printed book. As the author, I spend months selecting and experimenting with recipes and ingredients to develop the final concept. In our little town of Nelson B.C., I'm fortunate to have many talented people available to help me with the various stages in the overall process. I have heartfelt appreciation for each and every one of them who has assisted with the creation of this book.

Editing and proof reading a cookbook is a painstaking task and I'd like to shout out my thanks and extreme appreciation to Liz Abraham, Pete Lamb, Mya McLaughlin, Sarah Dobell, Margie Rosling, and to my family, Mike, Ali and Conner Adams. They read the recipes over and over again to make sure they are clear and organized so that our readers will have success in their kitchens. Their editing and critiques were essential.

The next stage is lots and lots of recipe testing! Our local stores make it possible to source all the best and freshest ingredients to use in the recipes. Thank you to Railway Station Meats and Deli, Fisherman's Market, Kootenay Co-op, Wing's Grocery, Ellison's Market, Flexy's Fruit Stand, Culinary Conspiracy and the Oyster Man.

I extend a giant thank you to Mya McLaughlin for testing and cooking her way through the entire book during the winter and spring of 2014. You've been an incredible help to me.

After all the recipe collecting, editing, proofing and testing comes the "pretty part": preparing all the recipes to be photographed, and making them look beautiful! The hugest heartfelt thank you to Amanda Skidmore, Emmy McKnight and Marianne Abraham for their professional and amazing combined talents in preparing the beautiful food and for doing the food styling and photo sets with me.

There's a kaleidoscope of props used in the staging of the photo shoots, so thanks also to Bella Flora, Prospero Pottery, Mellifera Bees, Okanagan Block, Lillie and Cohoe Hats, Wooden Bowls, Maison, Kootenai Moon Home, Kurama Sushi, Cottonwood Kitchens, Enso Hair Salon and Jaqueline Costa.

Thanks to the talented Laurel Colins for helping to create the dreamy dining scene. So pretty!

Thank you to the amazingly talented David Gluns who has worked with me for nine years and photographed for four cookbooks. We're a great team - Dave is patience personified and has the most creative energy and artistic eye for food shots. He is responsible for bringing all the recipes to life.

I would like to say "Merci beaucoup" to Dale Nigel Goble and Lynette Sawyer for the beautiful design and layout of Whitewater Cooks with Passion. Gorgeous!

For Minn Bennedict, who created the winning designs of the first three books - a bouquet of gratitude. Thanks Minny!

Thank you to Nancy Wise of Sandhill Book Marketing for her book industry advice, copywriting and editing of the back cover and preface sections and also for the terrific job Sandhill has done in promoting and distributing my books over the years.

Another note of thanks to all the retailers out there who have supported, promoted and hand sold my books to the general public. Without you, my books would never have reached the thousands of homes across Canada and the US that they have.

Big hugs to my sister Clare, first for being my dear sister – and for collaborating on the writing of the introduction page.

To end, I'd like to thank the person who started it all. On a snowy day in the winter of 2006 at Whitewater Ski Resort, my enthusiastic friend Lori McGinnis suggested I write a cookbook with all the most loved recipes from the Fresh Tracks Café. She offered to type and help in any way possible. And that she did! And because of her great idea nine years ago, three more books have been published and a cult-like following has begun! Thank you so much to Lori McGinnis!

Shelley

contents

breakfast

ali's granola

Here is an updated granola recipe that brings coconut oil and flax seeds into your morning ritual. Ali Adams is my very health conscious daughter and she shared this flavourful and fast to prepare bowl of goodness.

Makes 8 cups

ingredients

2 1/2 cups large flake oats

1 cup pecans, chopped roughly

1/2 cup almonds, chopped roughly

1/2 cup flax seeds

1 cup pumpkin seeds

1 cup sunflower seeds

1/2 cup unsweetened coconut ribbons or large flake unsweetened coconut

3 tbsp coconut oil

3 tbsp maple syrup

3 tsp cinnamon

1 cup dried goji or blueberries

method

Preheat oven to 325°F.

Mix oats, pecans, almonds, flax seeds, pumpkin seeds, sunflower seeds and coconut ribbons in a large mixing bowl.

Mix coconut oil, maple syrup and cinnamon together in a small pot and heat until melted and add to oat mixture.

Place granola mixture on baking tray and bake for 30 – 40 minutes, stirring a few times.

Remove from oven and let cool.

Add the berries and store in an airtight container.

Here is a fun idea for you die-hard fresh trackers or anyone needing a quick start morning. Layer granola, yogurt and berries in a glass canning jar and top with a lid and store in the fridge overnight. Grab it in the morning and eat it on the run! Don't forget your spoon!

chai tea

Are you tired of buying the boxed version of traditional chai tea? Here is the "good as it gets" homemade adaptation of what you might find on a street corner in India.

Makes 4 – 5 cups

ingredients

4 cups cold water

10 cardamom seeds, smashed open

6 whole cloves

1/2 inch piece fresh ginger, unpeeled

2 sticks of cinnamon

2 tbsp sugar (to taste)

2 bags good quality black tea

2/3 cup half and half cream, rice or soy milk

method

Place cold water in pot.

Add all ingredients except tea and cream.

Boil spices together for 3 – 5 minutes, depending on how spicy and strong you like it.

Add tea bags and turn heat to minimum. Let steep for 4 minutes.

Add cream and heat on low until tea is hot.

Add a shot of espresso to your cup of chai to turn it into a "Dirty Chai" and really feel the boost!

baked fruity breakfast oatmeal

How about dressing up plain oatmeal with this delicious and healthy baked version that is chock full of fruit, nuts and maple syrup. It is a fantastic and different version of the old classic. Kind of like eating a fruit crisp for breakfast!

Serves 6-8

ingredients

2 cups large flake oats

1/2 cup walnuts, toasted

1 tsp baking powder

1 1/2 tsp cinnamon

1/2 tsp salt

1/3 cup maple syrup

2 cups whole milk (you can substitute with almond or rice milk)

1 egg

3 tbsp butter, melted

1 tsp vanilla

2 bananas, ripe and sliced length-wise

1 1/2 cups frozen or fresh blueberries or any other berries you have on hand (or chopped apples and pears)

method

Preheat oven to 375°F.

Grease an 8 x 8 inch rectangular or oval ovenproof baking dish.

Mix together oats, walnuts, baking powder, cinnamon and salt in a large bowl.

Whisk together maple syrup, milk, egg, half the melted butter and vanilla in a separate bowl.

Arrange banana slices in the bottom of the baking dish and sprinkle 2/3 of the berries over them.

Cover the fruit mixture with the oat mixture.

Pour the milk mixture over the oats, tipping the pan a bit so that milk runs through the oat mix.

Scatter remaining berries over the top.

Bake for 35 – 40 minutes until the top is nicely golden and oatmeal has set.

Remove from oven and drizzle with remaining melted butter.

Serve it with your favourite yogurt and a few more berries. An awesome way to start the day for your gang heading off to spend a day in the fresh air or in school!

spanish frittata

This frittata is based on the traditional Spanish recipe for "Tortilla" filled with potatoes, onions and eggs. Hearty, flavourful and wheat free, it makes a fine choice for breakfast, brunch or lunch.

Serves 6-8

ingredients

2 tbsp olive oil

1 cup onions, diced finely

1/2 lb small nugget potatoes, sliced into very thin rounds (about two cups)

1 tsp sea salt

1 bunch asparagus, bases trimmed and cut into 1 inch lengths

1 red pepper, diced

1 cup artichoke hearts, drained and chopped coarsely (optional)

10 eggs, well beaten

2 tbsp fresh herbs, chopped, such as basil, parsley, dill, oregano, thyme or rosemary or any combination

1/2 cup feta or goat cheese, crumbled

2 tbsp olive oil

method

Preheat oven to 350°F.

Heat 2 tbsp oil in 10 inch ovenproof frying pan.

Add onions and potato slices and sauté on medium heat until potatoes are just cooked.

Sprinkle with sea salt.

Add asparagus, red pepper and artichoke hearts and sauté another 2 minutes until "al dente".

Whisk eggs and add fresh herbs.

Pour into skillet with the sautéed vegetables.

Cook over low heat until eggs are starting to set, about 5 minutes.

Top with feta or goat cheese.

Place pan in oven and cook for 15 minutes or until set.

Turn oven up to broil and cook a bit more until top starts to brown.

Remove from oven.

Drizzle with olive oil and serve warm.

There are many different vegetable combinations you could use in this versatile recipe. Check your market for your favourites! Try cauliflower for the veggie part and add curry for the spice. For a meat or seafood variation, try sliced chorizo sausage, smoked salmon or dungeness crab.

huevos rancheros

Once you make this spicy and versatile ranchero sauce, you will be glad to have it on hand. The masa harina really gives it those authentic flavours of Mexico. It is great in all your enchiladas, tacos, quesadillas and, of course, our Huevos!

Serves 2

ingredients

Ranchero Sauce

2 tbsp vegetable oil

1/2 onion, diced

6 garlic cloves, crushed and chopped

4 tbsp masa harina (corn masa flour)

2 tbsp ancho chili powder

1/2 tsp cumin

1 tsp salt

1/2 tsp pepper

1 tbsp dried oregano

4 cups vegetable stock, heated

2 tbsp tomato paste

1 tsp brown sugar

Huevos

1 tbsp butter or oil

1/2 cup Ranchero Sauce

1/2 cup monterey jack cheese, grated

2 - 8 inch tortillas, corn or flour

4 eggs, lightly beaten

1/2 cup salsa

2 tbsp sour cream

2 tbsp cilantro, chopped

Frijos

1 – 14 oz can pinto or black beans, drained and rinsed

1 tsp chipotle sauce

1 tsp balsamic vinegar

1 tsp brown sugar

1/2 tsp salt

method

Ranchero Sauce

Heat oil in a large saucepan over medium high heat.

Add onion and sauté for 2 -3 minutes until soft.

Add garlic and cook for another 3 minutes.

Sprinkle in the masa harina and stir constantly for a few seconds as it turns golden brown.

Add chili powder, cumin, salt, pepper and oregano and stir for 2 minutes.

Pour stock in slowly, whisking constantly to combine and bring to a boil.

Reduce to a simmer and whisk in the tomato paste and brown sugar.

Simmer partially covered for 20 – 30 minutes, stirring often.

Cool and store in mason jar or a container with a tight fitting lid in the fridge.

Frijos

Place beans, chipotle sauce, balsamic vinegar, brown sugar and salt in small saucepan over low heat and keep warm.

Huevos

Heat 2 medium frying pans over medium high heat.

Brush both pans with oil or butter.

Heat one tortilla in each pan.

Spoon 3 tbsp of Ranchero Sauce all over each tortilla.

Sprinkle one half of each tortilla with the cheese and the frijos.

Scramble eggs in a third small frying pan until cooked.

Place eggs on beans and cheese and fold tortilla in half.

Serve with your favourite salsa, sour cream and fresh chopped cilantro.

Fresh spinach can be added for some extra greens and, of course, bacon if you desire!
The recipe makes 6 cups of Ranchero Sauce so you will have lots left for your next Mexican creation.

tuscan eggs florentine

This dish is a wheat free alternative to the traditional Eggs Florentine. The eggs are cooked right in the spinach with a drizzle of cream. No English muffin, tons of healthy spinach and the method is easy so you can eat this for breakfast any day of the week.

Serves 2

ingredients

3 tbsp butter

6 cups fresh spinach or kale or a combination of both, chopped coarsely

1/2 tsp nutmeg

1 tsp sea salt

1/2 tsp pepper

1/2 cup whipping cream

4 eggs

4 tbsp parmesan, freshly grated

method

Preheat oven to 375° F.

Melt butter in a large ovenproof frying pan or baking dish on medium high heat.

Add spinach and cook until wilted, about 3 minutes.

Stir in nutmeg, salt and pepper.

Pour cream carefully to saturate the spinach and make 4 indentations into the mixture.

Crack one egg into each indentation.

Sprinkle the whole dish with parmesan.

Bake for 15 – 20 minutes or until eggs have set and the whole dish is bubbling.

You could add a layer of grilled tomatoes or prosciutto on top of the spinach for a great addition.

petie's red quinoa breakfast

Petie is one of my sporty friends who is a healthy eater and a very busy girl. Petie sometimes mixes the quinoa, milk and water together the night before and then turns it on when she gets up. It's ready to eat when she is finished showering and out the door she flies!

Serves 4

ingredients

1 cup red quinoa

1 cup water

1 cup almond milk, soy milk or coconut milk (or any combo of these)

1/2 tsp cinnamon

2 tbsp almond butter

2 cups fresh or frozen berries – raspberries are a favourite!

1/3 cup pecans, toasted

2 cups Greek yogurt

2 tbsp maple syrup

method

Combine quinoa, water and milk in a medium saucepan.

Bring to a boil over high heat and reduce to medium low.

Cover and cook for 20-25 minutes or until liquid has been absorbed.

Stir in the cinnamon and almond butter

Divide among 4 bowls and top with berries, pecans and a dollop of your favourite yogurt.

Drizzle with maple syrup to taste.

You can top this crunchy bowl of goodness with toasted coconut, chia seeds, flax seeds, chopped apples, whatever grabs you!

gail's oatmeal blueberry pancakes

Gail Morrison is heard before she is seen! She is always laughing!!! Her contagious laugh is the characteristic of what her spirit is, jovial, cheerful and positive, always. We LOVE Gail. She is a treasured friend from Whistler and we love everything Gail cooks.

Serves 6

ingredients

2 cups large flake oats

2 1/2 cups buttermilk

1/4 cup butter, melted and cooled

2 eggs, lightly beaten

1/2 cup whole wheat, white or non wheat flour

2 tbsp sugar

1 tsp baking powder

1 tsp baking soda

1/4 tsp salt

2 cups blueberries, fresh or frozen

method

Combine oats and buttermilk in a large bowl and let sit 15 – 30 minutes, the longer the better, even overnight.

Mix the cooled butter and eggs together in a small bowl and stir into oats and buttermilk.

Combine flour, sugar, baking powder, baking soda and salt in a separate bowl.

Add dry ingredients to egg and buttermilk mixture. Let rise for 10 minutes.

Fry pancakes on medium heat for about 3-5 minutes until first side is golden.

Sprinkle blueberries onto uncooked surface and then flip to cook the other side and cook for another minute or two.

Any uneaten pancakes are great the next day, toasted in the toaster with butter and honey or turned into a recess snack filled with PB and J.

croissant french toast with honeyed cranberries and brie

Okay, we agree that this is a little decadent, but every now and again it's so nice to really pull out all the stops for a festive brunch with friends or for your loved one on a cozy Sunday morning....

Serves 6

ingredients

2 tbsp butter

2 cups fresh or frozen cranberries

1/3 cup honey

3 eggs

2/3 cup milk

1 tsp vanilla

1 tbsp butter

6 croissants, sliced open

1/3 lb (150 g) brie, sliced thinly

method

Melt 2 tbsp butter in a small pot on medium heat and add cranberries.

Add honey and cook for 10 minutes until honey has thickened and berries have softened.

Beat eggs, milk and vanilla together in a shallow bowl.

Heat 1 tbsp butter until bubbling in a non-stick pan on medium heat.

Dip both croissant halves into egg mix, coating both sides well.

Fry for 3 – 5 minutes per side, until golden.

Place the sliced brie on bottom half of the croissants and let melt slightly.

Set the brie side of croissant on serving plate and ladle with warm cranberry sauce and top with the other half of the croissant.

Garnish with another dollop of cranberry sauce.

Cranberries are possibly the most complimentary tart fruit. Paired with sweet honey and savory brie, this dish covers all the flavour bases. To take it one step further add a few slices of prosciutto on top of the brie. Wow! Strawberries are amazing if cranberries are not your thing.

hello world smoothie

This morning smoothie is delicious and a perfect way to get half the servings of the daily recommended fruits and veggies without even noticing! It will keep you going and going and going!

Serves 2 (2 cups each)

ingredients

1/2 avocado

2 cups spinach leaves

1 medium kale or swiss chard leaf

1 cup frozen blueberries or raspberries

4 tbsp Big Omega 3 Seed mix, ground (see next page)

1 serving protein powder of your choice

1/2 cup anti-oxidant juice (pomegranate or acai)

1 cup almond milk, unsweetened

method

Place all ingredients in a blender and blend until very smooth.

This smoothie is also a great recovery drink after a long hike or bike ride.

big omega 3 seed mix

This mix of seeds contains all of the Omega 3 oils that we need to keep our skin smooth, our hair shiny and our brains sharp! Keep the seed mix in a jar and just grind enough for a few days use at a time. Put it in your smoothie or sprinkle it on your cereal. Energizing!

Makes 6 cups

ingredients

1 1/2 cups golden flax seeds, raw

1 1/2 cups hemp hearts

1/2 cup chia seeds

1/2 cup sesame seeds, raw

1 cup sunflower seeds, raw

1 cup pumpkin seeds, raw

method

Combine all ingredients in a large mixing bowl and mix well.

Store in an airtight container in the fridge or freezer.

Grind just enough for a few days at a time to ensure freshness.

Sprinkle at least 2 tbsp of ground seed mix per person into your smoothie or granola every day.

Packed full of healthy stuff, use whole (before grinding) and lightly toasted, on your green salads or steamed vegetables.

buckwheat waffles with fresh ricotta and citrus

These waffles are super healthy and a gorgeous earthy colour and flavour. It is fun to go beyond the usual waffles and try something a little different.

Serves 6

ingredients

1 cup buckwheat flour

1 cup all purpose flour

1/4 cup sugar

1 1/2 tsp baking powder

1/2 tsp sea salt

1 1/2 cups milk

1/4 cup butter, melted and cooled

1 large egg

1 1/2 cups fresh ricotta

2 blood oranges, peel and pith removed and sliced

1 grapefruit, peel and pith removed and sliced

4 clementines, peel and pith removed and sliced

honey or maple syrup for drizzling

method

Whisk together flours, sugar, baking powder and sea salt in a large mixing bowl.

Whisk together milk, melted butter and egg until well combined in a medium bowl.

Stir milk mixture into flour mixture until just combined. Let batter sit uncovered for 20 minutes.

Preheat a waffle iron and lightly coat with cooking spray.

Cook waffles until golden brown and crisp, about 8 minutes.

Serve with a spoonful of ricotta and slices of citrus.

Drizzle with honey or maple syrup.

Ricotta is so creamy and light and really goes well with the citrus. If you can't find ricotta, try mascarpone cheese or crème fraiche

starters

Oysters Motoyaki **26**

Haloumi Cheese with Creamy Tahini Sauce **28**

Sauteéd Garlic Goat Brie **29**

Grilled Squid Puttanesca **30**

Polenta Crostini **32**

Sagankai Prawns **33**

Grilled Pear and Chevre Crostini with Truffled Honey Drizzle **34**

Chickpea Flatbread **36**

Indian Artichoke Hummus **37**

Kim's Kale Chips **38**

Roasted Chickpea Tapas **38**

Star Anise Duck Cones with Avocado Wasabi Cream **41**

Lettuce Cups with Spicy Shrimp and Glass Noodles **44**

Yoshis Oshizushi **46**

Lamb Meatballs with Cinnamon and Pomegranate Jewels **48**

Braised Fresh Artichokes **50**

oysters motoyaki

We are so lucky to have such amazing fresh oysters here on the west coast of B.C. In our little town of Nelson, Brent Petkau blesses us with Island-to-the-Kootenays delivery, with bounties of fresh oysters and clams. Just when you are craving your next oyster fix, there he is, with his rosy cheeks, gumboots and French tam standing on the street corner with his offerings fresh from the sea.

Serves 4 - based on 3 oysters per person

ingredients

12 fresh oysters, rinsed and scrubbed

1 cup mayonnaise

1/4 cup green onions, chopped finely

1 tbsp miso paste

1 tsp sambal oelek (chili garlic sauce)

1 lemon, juice of

1 red pepper, roasted and finely diced

1/2 cup candied smoked salmon, shredded

method

Preheat oven to 425°F.

Shuck rinsed oysters, make sure you separate the oyster from the shell.

Place oysters still in their half shells on a baking sheet facing up on a bed of sea salt to keep them from sliding around.

Combine mayonnaise, green onions, miso paste, sambal oelek and lemon juice in a small bowl.

Coat each oyster with about 2 tsp of the sauce.

Top with diced red pepper and candied smoked salmon.

Bake for 7-8 minutes.

Serve with a lemon wedge.

Try these oysters with or without the red peppers and salmon , both ways are delectable!

haloumi cheese with creamy tahini sauce

Haloumi is a traditional cheese from the island of Cyprus in the Mediterranean. It has a higher melting point than most other cheeses, which makes it so suitable for grilling and frying. Drizzled with creamy tahini sauce and served with a cold beer, this starter makes a great beginning to any dinner.

Serves 4

ingredients

Tahini Sauce

1/2 cup tahini

2 lemons, zest of one and juice of both

2 garlic cloves, crushed and chopped

1/2 tsp salt

2 tsp cumin

1/2 - 3/4 cup water

1/2 cup fresh parsley, chopped

1/2 pound (250 g) haloumi cheese, sliced into 1/2 inch slices

2 tbsp olive oil

2 tbsp fresh dill or mint or oregano, chopped

method

Place tahini, lemon zest and juice, garlic, salt and cumin in a blender or food processor and pulse to combine.

Slowly drizzle in water until desired thickness is achieved.

Add parsley and process until just combined.

Pour into jar or bowl and store in fridge until ready to use.

Brush cheese with olive oil and fry on medium-high heat until crispy and brown, about 2 minutes per side.

Transfer to serving platter and sprinkle with fresh dill, mint or oregano.

Drizzle with Tahini Sauce.

Serve with grilled pita triangles, kalamata olives and grilled lemon halves.

The Cypriots like to serve their grilled haloumi with slices of cool fresh watermelon and lots of fresh mint. So refreshing!

sautéed garlic goat brie

This appetizer is ALL about decadence and a superb blend of textures. Deliberately simple, this recipe showcases the rich flavour of the goat brie.

Serves 4-6

ingredients

3 tbsp butter

1 egg white, lightly beaten

2 cloves garlic, crushed and chopped

1/2 cup panko breadcrumbs

one 6-8 inch round goat or regular brie cheese

method

Melt butter in a heavy bottomed sauté pan on medium heat until bubbling.

Place beaten egg white in a shallow bowl.

Mix garlic and panko crumbs together in another shallow bowl.

Dip brie in egg white and then into garlic and panko mixture.

Sauté in bubbling butter until golden brown, about 3 minutes. Flip over with large spatula and repeat.

Remove brie from pan and place on serving platter.

Cool and let brie set for 7 – 8 minutes before cutting into it.

Keep the presentation of this gorgeous brie simple. Garnish with fresh berries and colourful jellies such as the Jalapeno Pepper Jelly from Whitewater Cooks, pure, simple and real. Serve with crackers and a baguette.

grilled squid puttanesca

Serve this exquisite squid on top of our Polenta Crostini on page 32, or with a loaf of your favourite bread.

Serves 4

ingredients

1/2 lb (400 g package) squid tubes cut into 1 inch rings

1 tsp garlic, crushed and chopped

1 tbsp jalapeno pepper, seeded and diced finely

1 tbsp olive oil

1/2 tsp nutmeg

1/2 cup butter

1/2 cup fresh tomatoes, diced

1 lemon , zest and juice of

2 tbsp anchovy paste

1/4 cup capers

1/2 cup kalamata olives, pitted and chopped roughly

2 cloves garlic, crushed and chopped

1/4 cup red onion, diced

2 lemons, quartered for garnish

1/2 cup parsley, chopped

method

Marinate squid in garlic, jalapeno, olive oil and nutmeg for 30 minutes.

Preheat barbeque to medium heat.

Melt butter in sauté pan and cook on medium-low temperature until slightly browned.

Add tomatoes, lemon zest and juice, anchovy paste, capers, olives, garlic and red onions.

Sauté for another 2 minutes and then turn off heat.

Grill squid on heated barbeque for 2 minutes per side and add to warm sauce.

Garnish with lemon quarters and chopped parsley.

To get all the good bits, you will definitely need a fork and spoon!

polenta crostini

This alternative to baguette crostini hails from Italy and brings a wheat-free platform to the appetizer world. For delectable toppers, we've got a few suggestions on pages 30 and 33.

Makes 24 pieces

ingredients

6 cups water

2 cups vegetable stock

1 tsp salt

2 cups cornmeal

1/2 cup sun-dried tomatoes, chopped finely

3 tbsp fresh rosemary or basil, chopped finely

2/3 cup feta or goat cheese, crumbled

3 tbsp olive oil

method

Place water, vegetable stock and salt in a large, heavy-bottomed pot and heat to boiling.

Add cornmeal gradually, whisking constantly to prevent lumps.

Switch to a wooden spoon and stir the cornmeal for about 10 minutes on medium low heat until it is thick and there is a thin residue on the bottom of the pot. The mixture should be slowly bubbling this whole time.

Turn off heat and stir in sun-dried tomatoes, rosemary or basil and feta or goat cheese.

Spread polenta mixture onto a parchment lined 9x13 inch baking sheet and spread evenly to the edges of the baking sheet.

Place another piece of parchment paper over the polenta and press down gently to smooth out and flatten.

Cool and allow to set for at least 2 hours in the fridge or in a cool place.

Cut the polenta into 24 pieces and brush both sides with olive oil.

Preheat barbeque to medium high heat.

Grill polenta crostini for about 3-5 minutes per side until grill marks appear.

For a stress free dinner hour, make these crostinis earlier in the day and store on a platter, loosely covered with a tea towel, until assembly time.

saganaki prawns

This recipe was in *Whitewater Cooks with Friends,* but we wanted to share it again with a slightly different method. Plus, it goes so well as a topping with the Polenta Crostini on page 32.

Serves 6

ingredients

3 tbsp olive oil

1 medium yellow onion, sliced thinly

4 cloves garlic, crushed and chopped

1/2 tsp chili flakes

6 medium tomatoes, diced

1 cup fire roasted tomatoes* or canned diced tomatoes with liquid

1/2 cup ouzo or sambuca

1 tsp dried oregano

1 tsp pepper

1 lemon, juice of

1/2 cup fresh basil, chopped

1 bag (400 g) prawns, thawed and peeled, head and tails off (B.C. spot prawns are the best)

1/2 cup feta cheese, crumbled

method

Heat oil in wok or sauté pan.

Add onion and garlic and sauté until soft, about 5 minutes.

Add chili flakes and tomatoes and cook until slightly reduced, about 10 minutes.

Add ouzo, oregano, pepper, lemon juice and basil and cook for another 3 minutes.

Add prawns to sauce and cook until done, about 10-12 minutes (prawns will turn pink).

Arrange polenta crostini on serving plates, top with prawns and some of the tomato sauce and sprinkle with crumbled feta.

*fire roasted tomatoes can be found at Railway Station Meats and Deli and most specialty food stores.

The prawns are best served on individual plates on top of the polenta crostini but are also great along side some warm pita bread.

grilled pear and chevre crostini with truffled honey drizzle

A simple and uncomplicated starter for any dinner. Andrea and her French boyfriend Gilbert shared this crostini with us one cozy evening at their Kootenay Lake house. We added the truffled honey drizzle to jazz it up a little and it was absolutely delicious!

Serves 4

ingredients

1 sourdough baguette, sliced into 1/2 inch thick diagonal pieces (crostini)

1/4 cup extra virgin olive oil

1 garlic clove, peeled and halved

1/3 cup honey

2 tsp truffle oil

2 semi ripe pears, unpeeled, cored and sliced lengthwise into 8 slices

1 tbsp olive oil

2 tsp fresh lemon juice

5 oz good quality chevre (goat cheese), crumbled

method

Preheat oven to 350°F.

Place crostini slices on baking tray and brush both sides with olive oil.

Bake for about 10-15 minutes, flipping once when the bottom side is golden brown.

Remove from oven and rub the topside of each crostini with the halved garlic clove.

Place the honey in a small bowl and place over a bain marie until honey loosens up.

Turn off the heat and whisk in the truffle oil and set aside. The mixture will turn slightly cloudy.

Heat a grill pan or barbeque to medium-high heat.

Brush the pears with olive oil and grill on both sides until grill marks appear.

Place on a plate and drizzle with lemon juice and set aside until needed.

Place the pears on top of the crostini slices.

Top with the crumbled goat cheese.

Bake in oven for 3-4 minutes, just to warm up and melt the cheese slightly.

Drizzle with the truffled honey.

If truffles are not your thing, substitute the truffle oil with hazelnut or any of your favourite oils to create your own infusion.

chickpea flatbread

Super easy to make, this delicious flatbread is versatile and gluten-free. Pair it with any of our dip recipes found in all the Whitewater cookbooks and especially the Artichoke Hummus on page 37 in this book. Making this in a 12 inch pizza pan produces the best results.

Serves 4 - 6   Makes one 12 inch pizza pan

ingredients

2 1/2 cups water

4 tbsp olive oil, divided

2 cups chickpea flour*

1 tsp cumin

1/2 - 1 tsp sea salt (plus extra for the top)

1/2 tsp pepper, freshly ground

method

Preheat oven to 425°F

Place water in a bowl with 1 tbsp of the olive oil.

Whisk in chickpea flour, cumin and salt gradually, until batter is smooth and creamy.

Cover and let stand at room temperature for at least 30 minutes.

Rub remaining 3 tbsp olive oil around the base and sides of one 12 inch non-stick pizza pan. It must be quite oily to get the crisp edges on the flatbread.

Stir the batter a few times and pour it onto the pizza pan.

Bake for 25-30 minutes or until set and golden brown.

Serve warm or at room temperature, sprinkled with coarse sea salt and pepper.

*Chickpea flour is available in the Asian food section of most grocery stores.

Serve flatbread cut into wedges or just leave it whole and let your guests tear into it!

indian artichoke hummus

Here's a new twist on the traditional hummus. The lovely aromas of India infuse this vegan dip. It goes perfectly with the chickpea flatbread on page 36 or pita crisps or papadums.

Makes 2 1/2 cups

ingredients

1 – 14 oz can artichoke hearts, drained

1 - 14 oz can chickpeas, drained and rinsed

1 tbsp rice vinegar

1 tbsp apple cider vinegar

2 tsp maple syrup

2 tbsp tamari sauce

2 tsp garam masala

1 tsp fresh ginger, peeled and grated

1 tsp nutritional yeast

1/2 tsp salt

1/2 tsp pepper

method

Place all ingredients in food processor and blend until puréed and smooth.

Serve chilled.

Store in fridge for up to two weeks.

To make pita crisps, cut pitas in eighths, drizzle with olive oil in a large bowl and toss to coat evenly. Place on a baking sheet and bake for about 15 minutes, until crispy and brown.

kim's kale chips

Needing a healthy and different little tapas snack? Kim Irving is a Nelson gal who is really sporty and humourous and knows a great little snack when she sees one. The perfect crunch with loads of flavour!

Serves 4

ingredients

2 bunches kale, rinsed, stems removed and ripped

into "chip-sized" pieces

2 tbsp olive oil or coconut oil

1 tbsp sea salt

method

Preheat oven to 350°F.

Toss kale pieces with olive oil and massage oil in with your fingers.

Sprinkle with sea salt and spread on a baking sheet.

Bake for 15 – 20 minutes.

Check after 15 minutes for crispness.

Remove from oven and let cool.

Try adding other seasonings like black pepper, yeast flakes, toasted sesame seeds, seasoning salt or dill to switch up the flavours.

roasted chickpea tapas

Lower in fat than nuts and healthier for you than chips, these tasty little snacks are fast and easy to make. Keep a jar of these on hand to accompany your aperitif hour.

Serves 4

ingredients

2 – 19 oz cans of chickpeas, rinsed, drained and dried on a tea towel

3 tbsp olive oil

1 tbsp curry powder

1 tsp paprika

1 tbsp garlic, crushed and chopped

1/4 tsp cayenne pepper

1 tbsp dried dill

2 tsp sea salt

1/2 tsp pepper, freshly ground

method

Preheat oven to 400°F.

Place chickpeas on a parchment lined baking tray.

Bake for 10 minutes, then shake them around and bake for another 5 minutes until crisp.

Transfer chickpeas to mixing bowl and add olive oil, curry powder, paprika, garlic, cayenne, dill, salt and pepper and toss until chickpeas are coated.

Spread out on the baking sheet and roast for a further 3-5 minutes until fragrant.

Remove from oven and let cool.

Toss on your salad or on soup for some added crunch.

WHITEWATER COOKS
pure, simple, and real creations.

star anise duck cones with avocado wasabi cream

You will be dazzled by the taste and beauty of these mouth-watering crunchy cones. Heat resistant fingertips come in handy for the preparation!

Serves 10 (2 cones per person)

ingredients

2 whole duck breasts, boneless and skin on

Marinade

2 tbsp red onion, diced finely

2 tbsp fresh ginger, peeled and grated

1/4 tsp Chinese 5 spice

1 orange, juice and zest of

8 whole star anise

1/4 cup soy sauce

1/4 cup sweet chili sauce

1/2 tsp sesame oil

1 tbsp brown sugar

1 tbsp sesame oil

1 tbsp vegetable oil

1 tsp cornstarch mixed with 2 tsp water

method

Marinade

Cut cross marks into the fat cap on the top layer of the duck breasts.

Whisk together the onion, ginger, 5 spice, orange juice and zest, star anise, soy sauce, sweet chilli sauce, sesame oil and brown sugar in a glass bowl and immerse duck breast in marinade for at least 2 hours in fridge.

Preheat oven to 400°F.

Drain duck breast, pat dry with paper towel and save marinade removing star anise.

Heat sesame and vegetable oil in a medium sized pan on high.

Sear duck, skin side down, until skin is crisp and juice begins to seep out, about 3 – 5 minutes.

Finish by roasting duck uncovered in oven for 15 minutes.

Cool duck breast and then chill thoroughly, at least 30 minutes.

Slice duck breast diagonally across the grain – you will get about 20 thin slices – set aside.

Heat marinade to a light boil, add cornstarch/water mixture and whisk until thickened – set aside.

Recipe continued on next page

ingredients

Cones

1/3 cup corn syrup

1 tsp miso paste

1/2 tsp sesame oil

1 tsp ground ginger

4 tbsp black sesame seeds

4 tbsp sesame seeds, toasted

1/2 cup pastry flour

1 tbsp butter, room temperature

Avocado Wasabi Cream

1 avocado, ripe and mashed

1/2 cup cream cheese

1 tbsp wasabi paste

1/2 tsp soy sauce

1 cup arugula, chopped coarsely

method

Cones

Preheat oven to 400°F.

Combine corn syrup, miso paste, sesame oil, ginger and both sesame seeds and mix well

Cut butter into pastry flour with a fork until blended evenly. Add the flour mixture to the corn syrup mixture and combine well.

Line two baking sheets with parchment paper, have one sheet handy to make the next batch on a cool tray

Starting with 1 tbsp of batter for each circle, spread thinly into 4 - four inch circles on a baking sheet with a small metal spatula or the back of a soupspoon, dipped repeatedly in cool water.

Bake for approximately 7-8 minutes until golden brown. **Make** 4 more circles on the second baking sheet while first is baking.

Quickly peel off the rounds and wrap around a cone mold or the handle of a wooden spoon while still hot, you will have about 2 minutes until they cool off.

Repeat cone wrapping process with remaining baked rounds – if they get too hard to wrap, pop them back in the oven to soften them up again for about 30 seconds.

Twist cone molds out of the hardened cones and use for next set of baked rounds.

Avocado Wasabi Cream

Combine avocado, cream cheese, wasabi paste and soy sauce in a medium sized bowl and blend with hand mixer.

Pipe or spoon avocado cream into cooled cones until 1/2 full.

Top with 2 slices duck breast, arugula and a drizzle of cooled marinade.

Arrange on a sea salt lined platter for serving so the cones stand up!

For another amazing version of this appetizer, try these cones filled with Ahi Tuna Tartare from Whitewater Cooks At Home. You could also make this recipe by buying a Peking Duck at a Chinese grocer and shredding or slicing the already cooked and seasoned duck. Cone molds can be purchased at Cottonwood Kitchens or fine cooking stores.

lettuce cups with spicy shrimp and glass noodles

This is an incredibly tasty noodle salad and is a really fun and light way to start a dinner party. You can use any type of noodles you like. Buckwheat soba noodles taste great and this would also make this a wheat-free choice.

Serves 6

ingredients

1 large head iceberg or butter lettuce, leaves separated

1/2 cup rice vinegar

3 tbsp sugar

1/2 tsp salt

2 cloves garlic, crushed and chopped

1/2 fresh red chili, seeded and chopped finely

1 tsp sesame oil

1 lime, zest and juice of

2 tbsp chili paste

2 tsp sesame oil

2 tsp chives or green onions, chopped finely

2 cups cooked shrimp meat

1/2 cup vegetable oil

1 large eggplant, diced into 3/4 inch cubes

1/2 tsp salt

1 package (9 oz) glass noodles *

1 large mango, diced into 3/4 inch cubes

1 1/2 cups fresh basil, chopped

1 1/2 cups fresh cilantro, chopped

1/2 cup fresh mint, chopped

1/2 red onion, sliced thinly

1 1/2 cups peanuts, lightly toasted and chopped

method

Wash lettuce and store leaves in paper towel.

Place vinegar, sugar and 1/2 tsp salt in a small saucepan and gently heat until crystals dissolve.

Remove from heat and add garlic, chili and sesame oil.

Allow to cool and then add lime zest and juice.

Combine chili paste, sesame oil and chives in a small bowl. Add shrimp and marinate in fridge until needed.

Heat vegetable oil in a frying pan and sauté the eggplant cubes, turning occasionally until just tender and browned – about 8 to 10 minutes. You will have to do this in several batches.

Remove from heat, place in colander, sprinkle with 1/2 tsp salt and leave to drain.

Cook noodles according to package instructions.

Drain and rinse with cold water and lay the noodles on a clean tea towel to dry.

Toss noodles with the cooled dressing, cooked eggplant, diced mango, basil, cilantro, mint, red onions and chopped peanuts and place in a bowl. Lay shrimp on top and keep cool until serving.

Stack the lettuce leaves on a platter and place the salad beside it. Let guests make their own salad "taco" on individual plates.

* glass noodles are available at Wing's grocery or most Asian grocery stores.

yoshi's oshizushi

Our local Nelson Sushi master Yoshi of Kurama Sushi Restaurant shared this version of "pressed sushi ". It's easy to make ahead of time, even the night before which is always a good thing. Get as creative as you want with layers of different fish and veggies.

Serves 4-6

ingredients

100 g thinly sliced smoked salmon

4 cups cooked and cooled sushi rice (seasoned with 2 tbsp rice vinegar and 2 tbsp white sugar, heated until disolved)

2 small avocados, sliced*

2 tbsp fresh dill, chopped

2 lemons, peeled and sliced very thinly

One 5 x 9 1/2 x 1 inch high plastic or glass container or a Oshizushi Hako which is a wooden container made for making this pressed sushi.

method

Line plastic wrap on the bottom and up the sides of the container.

Place the smoked salmon slices in the bottom of the container covering completely.

Spread sushi rice on top of the salmon.

Layer avocado slices on top of rice.

Cover rice and avocado with plastic wrap and press evenly with the palm of your hand or with a hard flat object.

Remove plastic wrap and flip container upside down on a cutting board or serving platter.

Wipe the blade of a very sharp knife with a wet tea towel and cut Oshizushi into one inch slices.

Top with dill and lemon slices.

* if making this the night before, add the avocado layer just before serving.

Cucumbers, spicy mayonnaise, toasted sesame seeds, ahi tuna, nori and crab are all great layer ideas.
Douzo meshi agare!!! "Have a good meal! " in Japanese.

lamb meatballs with cinnamon and pomegranate jewels

We love a protein based appetizer and adore anything Mediterranean. The cinnamon and pomegranate seeds are such a sweet addition to these little lamb gems. Serve them with raita, your favourite chutney and lots of toothpicks.

Serves 4-6 (about 16 meatballs) 1 ounce each

ingredients

Meatballs

1 lb ground lamb

1/4 cup onion, diced finely

1 tbsp fresh mint, chopped

1 tbsp fresh cilantro, chopped

1 clove garlic, crushed and chopped

1 tsp coriander

1 tsp salt

1/2 tsp cinnamon

1/2 tsp allspice

1/2 tsp fresh or dried oregano, chopped if fresh

1/2 tsp pepper

1/2 cup pomegranate seeds

Raita

1 cup plain yogurt, Greek style

2 tsp fresh mint, chopped

2 tsp fresh cilantro, chopped

1 tsp cumin

1 lemon, zest of

method

Mix together lamb, onion, mint, cilantro, garlic, coriander, salt, cinnamon, allspice, oregano and pepper in a large mixing bowl until well combined.

Mix pomegranate seeds in until just incorporated.

Form mixture into 16 meatballs, place on a baking sheet and put in fridge until ready to cook.

Preheat oven to 400°F.

Bake meatballs in top third of oven for 15-20 minutes until brown.

Combine all raita ingredients and mix well and set aside in small bowl.

For a pretty presentation, serve these meatballs with raita and chutney on a bed of grape leaves. Grape leaves can be found in almost any specialty food store. They come in a bottle and you just unroll them and give them a little rinse. They are also edible if anyone wants some extra greens. Our Sun-Dried Tomato and Fennel Chutney is delicious with these and the recipe can be found in Whitewater Cooks pure simple, and real.

braised fresh artichokes

I love artichokes!! Everything about them!!! The beauty of them growing in the garden, the sensuous way of sharing them, all the ways they can be prepared, from steamed to grilled to deep fried to pureed to braised! Here is one of the many ways you can make and share one of my most adored vegetables.

Serves 2

ingredients

2 whole artichokes
2 lemons
1 1/2 cups dry white wine
1 cup water
1/2 cup extra virgin olive oil
1 tsp coarse sea salt

1/4 tsp red pepper flakes
5 cloves garlic, crushed and chopped
2 tbsp flat leaf parsley, chopped
1 tbsp fresh oregano, chopped
2 tbsp fresh mint, chopped

method

Preheat oven to 350°F.
Peel off tough outer leaves of artichokes.
Trim the bottom edge of the stem.
Trim pointy ends of the leaves on the artichoke with scissors.
Cut off the tops and then cut down the middle.
Trim out the choke (the hairy thing!) with a small spoon.
Place prepared artichokes in a large bowl of cold water with the juice of one of the lemons to keep from discolouring.
Drain artichokes and place cut side up in a wide ovenproof pot or casserole dish.

Pour wine, water, and olive oil over artichokes and sprinkle with salt, red pepper flakes, garlic and half of the fresh herbs.
Bring to a boil over high heat.
Cover artichokes with a sheet of parchment paper and then a lid or tinfoil.
Transfer to oven and braise until artichokes are tender and the leaves pull out easily, about 45 minutes.
Drizzle with a bit more olive oil, the juice of the remaining lemon and the remaining fresh herbs.
Serve in shallow bowls with the braising liquid.

Your favourite crusty baguette is a must to soak up the delicious braising liquid.
Thanks to my dear friend Michele for reminding me of just another way to share my love of artichokes.

soups

roasted garlic, carrot and cauliflower soup

This is a recipe from my dear friend Michele Repine whom I met in Paris at cooking school. We have kept in touch all these years and still cherish our time we spent together at La Varenne Ecole de Cuisine. This soup is comforting, light and creamy all at the same time.

Serves 6

ingredients

1 whole head garlic, separated into cloves, skins on

1 head cauliflower, broken into little florets

4 medium carrots, peeled and diced

1 tbsp olive oil

2 lemons, zest and juice of

1 tsp sea salt

1/2 tsp freshly ground black pepper

1 medium onion, diced

1 jalapeno pepper, seeded and diced

1 tbsp smoked Spanish paprika

2 cups vegetable stock

1 can coconut milk

1 tsp honey

1/2 cup slivered almonds, toasted

4 tbsp cilantro, chopped

method

Preheat oven to 400°F.

Place garlic cloves with skins on into 2 cups of water in a small saucepan and simmer for 15 minutes.

Drain garlic and reserve the water.

Crush garlic cloves with the back of a knife and discard the skins.

Combine cauliflower, carrots, garlic cloves, olive oil, lemon juice and zest, sea salt and pepper.

Roast on a cookie sheet for 20-30 minutes until lightly browned.

Sauté the onion in oil until soft, about 2 minutes and add the jalapeno and paprika and sauté for another minute.

Place roasted cauliflower, carrots, garlic, the onion mixture, vegetable stock and reserved water from garlic in food processor.

Puree until smooth - you might have to do this in two batches.

Return to pot, add coconut milk and honey and reheat.

Garnish with toasted almonds and cilantro.

The vibrant flavours of the roasted cauliflower, carrots and garlic make for a stunning side dish all on their own! Stop before processing and serve.

tana's borscht of all borschtness-ness's

Tana is a childhood friend that can always make me laugh and is a source of fun and crazy names for things. Like "Borscht of all Borschtness-ness's". This soup is FULL of vegetables and flavour and Tana says it is so good she could bathe in it too!

Serves 12

ingredients

3 tbsp grapeseed or safflower oil

2 onions, diced

3 garlic cloves, crushed and chopped

1 tsp fresh turmeric, peeled and grated or 1 tsp ground

2 tbsp paprika

1/2 tsp thyme

1 tsp cumin

3 carrots, peeled and diced

3 celery ribs, diced

1/2 purple cabbage, sliced thinly and chopped

3 parsnips, peeled and diced

4-6 small beets, peeled and diced

2-3 potatoes, peeled and diced

2 fennel bulbs, diced

1 can (28 oz) diced tomatoes, with liquid

3 tbsp tomato paste

12 cups (3 L) vegetable stock

2 bay leaves

1/4 cup fresh lemon juice

2 tbsp apple cider vinegar

1/4 cup golden raisins

1/4 cup brown sugar or honey

sea salt and pepper

1/4 cup fresh dill, chopped

plain yogurt or sour cream

fresh chives

method

Heat oil in a large heavy bottomed pot and sauté onions, garlic, turmeric, paprika, thyme, cumin, carrots, celery, cabbage, parsnips, beets, potatoes and fennel for about 10 minutes until vegetables are coated in the spices and just starting to brighten.

Add tomatoes, tomato paste, vegetable stock and bay leaves and bring to a boil.

Reduce heat and let simmer until vegetables are tender, about 15-20 minutes.

Add lemon juice, apple cider vinegar, raisins, brown sugar or honey and salt and pepper to taste. Simmer another 15 minutes.

Turn off heat and add fresh dill.

Garnish with yogurt or sour cream and chopped chives.

Add a bit of horseradish to the sour cream garnish for some kick.

honey miso roasted squash and soba noodle soup

Yum! Another great way to dish up one of our favourites, butternut squash. When roasted salty and sweet this way, the squash brings a distinctive flavour to the soup.

Serves 4

ingredients

2 cups butternut squash, peeled, seeded and cubed into 1 inch pieces

2 tbsp honey

2 tbsp brown rice miso, divided

1 tbsp rice vinegar

1 tbsp sesame oil

1 tbsp fresh ginger, grated

1/4 tsp cayenne pepper

1/4 cup sesame seeds

5 cups vegetable stock

1 hot cup water

4 five inch pieces of kombu*

1/3 cup bonito flakes *

1 cup shimeji or enoki mushrooms, whole (optional)

1 cup fresh spinach, chopped coarsely

4 oz buckwheat soba noodles, cooked and cooled

4 green onions, chopped

*kombu and bonito flakes can be found in most specialty food stores.

method

Preheat oven to 400°F.

Place cubed squash in large bowl.

Whisk together honey, 1 tbsp miso, rice vinegar, sesame oil, ginger and cayenne in a small pan and heat until melted.

Pour over squash and toss well.

Add sesame seeds and toss again.

Place on parchment lined baking sheet and roast in preheated oven for 15 – 20 minutes until al dente.

Heat vegetable stock, water and kombu in a large saucepan until boiling.

Turn off heat and add bonito flakes and let stand for 5 minutes.

Strain stock through a fine sieve into a bowl, discard kombu and bonito flake residue and return broth to pan.

Dissolve remaining 1 tbsp miso in 1 cup of hot water and stir back into stock.

Add squash and mushrooms and simmer for 2-3 minutes only and stir in spinach.

Place a little pile of cooled soba noodles in the bottom of each soup bowl and ladle broth and vegetables over top.

Garnish with chopped green onions.

Soba noodles are made from buckwheat, which is not wheat at all but comes from fruit seeds making this a fantastic wheat free soup.

moroccan vegetable soup with couscous

Morocco is one of the most festive and flavourful places in the world just like this soup!

Serves 6

ingredients

6 cups vegetable stock

4 - 6 carrots, peeled and sliced diagonally

1/2 large turnip, peeled and sliced diagonally into small pieces

3 tbsp olive oil

1/2 cup shallots, sliced thinly

1 tsp sea salt

1 tsp cumin

1 tsp ras el hanout (optional) *

1 tbsp harissa * or sambal oelek (more if you like it hot)

1/3 cup white wine

1 – 19 oz can chickpeas, rinsed and drained

1/4 tsp saffron

1 tsp honey

1 1/2cups couscous, cooked

1/2 cup cilantro or parsley, chopped

method

Place vegetable stock in large pot and bring to a boil.

Add carrots and turnips and simmer for 3 – 5 minutes until they turn a rich colour.

Drain vegetables and reserve the stock.

Place olive oil in a large pot and sauté shallots over medium heat until tender, about 5 minutes.

Add salt, cumin, ras el hanout and harissa, stirring constantly for about a minute.

Add wine and simmer for another minute.

Add cooked carrots and turnips, chickpeas, reserved vegetable stock and saffron to onion mixture.

Bring to a boil and reduce to a simmer until the carrots and turnips are tender, about 10 minutes.

Add honey and stir until dissolved.

Prepare couscous.

Divide cooked couscous into 6 bowls.

Ladle soup over couscous and garnish with chopped cilantro or parsley.

*Harissa is a Tunisian chili sauce available locally at Culinary Conspiracy or most specialty food stores.
*ras el hanout is a Moroccan spice blend made up of many spices and available at Culinary Conspiracy or most specialty food stores.

bengali chicken soup

This hearty India inspired soup makes an enticing main course on cold, rainy nights that need some heat and exotics! Fermented foods are proven to help with digestion, so the sauerkraut is an added bonus in this recipe.

Serves 6

ingredients

3 tbsp olive oil

1 large onion, diced

4 – 5 cloves garlic, crushed and chopped

1 1/2 tsp ground coriander

1 tsp curry powder

1 tbsp fresh ginger, peeled and grated

1/2 tsp dried red chili flakes

1 1/2 tsp turmeric

4 cups low sodium chicken stock

1-14 oz can coconut milk

1/2 cup jasmine rice, uncooked

2 cups sauerkraut, with liquid

1/2 cup carrots, peeled and sliced

1 cup potatoes, peeled and sliced

2 cups cooked chicken, shredded or sliced thinly

1/2 cup kecap manis*

1 cup cilantro, chopped

*available at most grocery stores in the Asian food section.

method

Sauté onions and garlic in oil on medium high heat in a large soup pot until soft.

Add coriander, curry powder, ginger, chili flakes and turmeric to onions and continue to sauté for another 2 minutes.

Add chicken stock, coconut milk, rice, sauerkraut, carrots, potatoes, chicken and kecap manis and bring to a boil.

Turn heat down to a simmer, cover and cook for 1 hour.

Stir in chopped cilantro and serve.

A barbequed chicken from your local supermarket works really well for this soup too and it is great served with chapatis or naan bread.

duck pho

This is a beautiful Vietnamese soup, shared by the adorable Barb Gosney who brought her amazing cooking skills with her from England. Pho is ALL about the stock so buy a whole roasted Peking Duck and use the carcass for the most wonderful flavour possible!

Serves 4

ingredients

1 Chinese roasted Peking Duck*

8 cups water or chicken stock or a combination of both

8 whole star anise

1 tsp black peppercorns

1/4 cup soy sauce

2 tbsp hoisin sauce

2 tbsp fish sauce

8 oz (1/2 package) vermicelli rice noodles

1 bunch fresh cilantro

1 small bunch mint

1 bunch (2 cups) fresh basil, Thai, if available

1 lb bean sprouts

1 small head of butter lettuce, separated into leaves

4 green onions, sliced

2 shallots, sliced thinly and fried until crispy

1/2 cup peanuts, roasted and chopped

1 nori sheet, julienned into thin strips

1 lime, quartered

1 red Thai chili, sliced, de-seeded and placed in a small bowl with fish sauce to cover

Recipe continued on next page

method

Remove all the meat from the duck and separate the skin and set aside.

Put duck carcass, water or stock, star anise and peppercorns in large pot and bring to a boil.

Reduce heat, cover and let simmer for 1 hour.

Strain stock through a large sieve or large coffee filter into a separate bowl. Discard bones, carcass, star anise and peppercorns.

Return stock to heat and keep warm.

Add soy sauce, hoisin and fish sauce.

Slice the duck meat and set aside.

Soak the rice noodles in boiling water until tender, about 4 minutes, drain and set aside.

De-stalk the herbs and tear into small pieces for garnishing the soup.

Place the duck skin on a baking sheet and crisp in oven for 10-15 minutes at 375°F.

Remove crisp skin, julienne and set aside.

Place equal amounts of rice noodles into each bowl.

Top with bean sprouts, sliced duck meat, lettuce leaves, green onions and herbs.

Ladle hot broth over top of each bowl.

Garnish with shallots, chopped peanuts, duck skin and nori strips.

Serve with lime wedges and red chilis soaked in fish sauce.

* sold at Wing's Grocery store and most Chinese markets.

Make sure you have some chopsticks and soupspoons, preferably the Chinese ones to accompany this gorgeous pho...

italian wedding soup

Don't you just love the name of this soup? It makes you feel festive and loved and eating it really makes you feel like an Italian mother has comforted you! The meatballs can be made ahead and frozen, the rest of this soup is just a simple preparation. Prego!

Serves 10-12

ingredients

Meatballs

1 pound organic ground beef
(or the meat from Italian sausages)

1/2 cup onion, diced finely

1 clove garlic, crushed and chopped

1/2 cup parmesan cheese, grated

1 tsp salt

1/2 cup panko crumbs (or polenta)

1 tsp dried basil

1 tsp parsley, chopped

1 egg

Soup

2 tbsp butter

1 medium onion, diced

2 medium carrots, diced

1 clove garlic, crushed and chopped

12 cups (3 litres) homemade or low sodium chicken stock

salt and pepper

1 cup Acini di Pepe*

1 lemon, juice of

1/2 cup marsala or red wine

1 pound fresh spinach, chopped

method

Preheat oven to 350°F.

Place beef, onion, garlic, parmesan, salt, panko crumbs, basil, parsley and egg in large bowl and mix with your hands to combine well.

Shape into tiny bite-sized meatballs and place onto a parchment lined baking sheet.

Roast meatballs for 15 minutes and set aside.

Melt butter in a large stockpot and add onion, carrots and garlic.

Sauté until tender, about 5 minutes.

Add chicken stock and bring to a boil.

Turn down to medium heat.

Add salt and pepper to taste.

Drop meatballs into broth and re-heat for 5 minutes.

Add Acini di Pepe and cook for 5 minutes.

Add lemon juice and marsala wine and heat another 5 minutes.

Add spinach and simmer for another few minutes until spinach is just cooked and still bright green.

Ladle into bowls and garnish with grated parmesan

* Acini di Pepe is Italian pasta in pearl sized balls that are perfect in this soup.

If you have any leftover parmesan rinds, adding them to the broth enhances the flavour.

artichoke vichyssoise
with olive tapenade

We love chilled soup, especially on a stinking hot day or any day!   When we discovered this recipe, we knew it was a keeper and the olive tapenade and a drizzle of extra virgin olive oil put it over the top!

Serves 4

ingredients

3 tbsp butter

2 cups leeks, chopped finely

1 can (398 ml) artichoke hearts, drained and chopped

1 large potato, peeled and diced

2 1/3 cups low sodium chicken stock

1/2 cup white wine

1 tbsp dried or fresh tarragon, chopped

1/4 tsp salt

1/4 tsp pepper

1 cup whipping cream

Olive Tapenade

1 cup kalamata olives, pitted

2 tbsp capers

3 tbsp parsley

2 cloves garlic

1 tbsp lemon zest

1/4 tsp salt

2 tbsp extra virgin olive oil

1 tomato, diced finely

extra virgin olive oil for drizzling

method

Melt butter in a large saucepan over medium-high heat.

Add leeks and artichokes and cook until leeks are soft, about 4 minutes.

Add potato, chicken stock and wine.

Bring to a boil, reduce heat to medium low.

Stir in tarragon and simmer, covered for 30 minutes.

Add salt and pepper and puree in a blender until very smooth. Place in a bowl or a juice jug.

Whisk in cream.

Cool in the fridge for 2-3 hours.

Place olives, capers, parsley, garlic, lemon zest, salt and olive oil in a food processor and pulse until combined but still slightly chunky.

Ladle chilled soup into serving bowls and top with olive tapenade, chopped tomato and a drizzle of extra virgin olive oil.

A pitcher of sangria is a great addition if the evening is especially hot!

salads

kale caesar

This is a tricky way to get some kale into your kids! Just a really good Caesar dressing, with half romaine lettuce and half fresh, healthy kale, that's all!

Serves 6

ingredients

1 head romaine lettuce, washed and chopped

2 cups kale, stem removed and chopped

1 egg

1 garlic clove

1 tsp salt

1 tsp pepper

1/4 tsp sugar

1/2 lemon, juice of

1 tsp anchovy paste

3/4 cup olive oil

1/4 cup parmesan or asiago, grated

2 tbsp capers, quickly sautéed in olive oil until crisp

method

Place romaine and kale in large salad bowl.

Put egg, garlic clove, salt, pepper, sugar, lemon juice and anchovy paste in food processor and process until blended.

Add olive oil and blend until smooth and thick.

Pour dressing over romaine and kale and toss.

Top with grated parmesan or asiago cheese.

Sprinkle crispy capers all over salad.

Add some croutons drizzled with truffle oil and lemon zest for fun or baked tofu cubes to keep it wheat free!

barley sushi salad

Tradional sushi flavours without all the work! This is a refreshing and nutritious salad that will quickly become a lunch favourite.

Serves 6

ingredients

2 cups water

3/4 cup pearl barley

10 shiitake mushroom caps cut into thin strips and sautéed until brown

1/2 cup smoked salmon lox, julienned

1/2 long english cucumber, seeded and diced

3 tbsp pickled ginger, chopped coarsely

4 tbsp rice vinegar

2 tsp sugar

4 tsp sesame oil

1 1/2 tsp wasabi paste

1/2 tsp salt

1 sheet nori, julienned into 2/3 inch strips

2 tbsp sesame seeds, toasted

method

Bring water to a boil.

Add barley and cook uncovered until tender – about 25 minutes.

Drain and rinse cooked barley under cold running water. Leave in colander to drain a further 10 minutes.

Transfer to a large salad bowl.

Add sautéed mushrooms, salmon, cucumber and pickled ginger to barley mix.

Whisk vinegar with sugar, sesame oil, wasabi paste and salt in small bowl.

Drizzle vinaigrette over barley mixture and stir until combined.

Stir 2/3 of the nori strips into the salad.

Garnish with remaining nori pieces and sesame seeds.

To make this more like a California roll, add a few slices of avocado!

tender beets and greens
with warm gorgonzola dressing

There is something about a warm dressing on a simple salad that does it for us! Substitute the beets with grilled pear slices for a nice change.

Serves 6

ingredients

Dressing

6 tbsp gorgonzola cheese, crumbled

1/4 cup white wine

2 tbsp olive oil

2 tbsp fresh rosemary, chopped finely

Salad

6 cups mesclun salad greens

3 medium sized beets, red, orange or yellow, cooked, peeled and sliced thinly*

3 heads Belgium endive, julienned

1/2 cup pecan pieces, toasted

method

Place gorgonzola, wine, olive oil and rosemary in a sauce pan and heat gently until combined and warm.

Place salad greens on individual plates or serving platter.

Top with the sliced beets and julienned endive.

Drizzle with warm gorgonzola dressing.

Top with pecans.

We like to cook our beets in the oven. Wrap them in tin foil and place in a baking dish. They take about 40 minutes depending on the size of the beets. Remove the tinfoil and cut the top and bottom ends off the beets and slip off the skins.

kale and brussels sprouts salad

Thanks to Sheri, my friend whose favourite thing to do is play hockey, for sharing this recipe. She loves to make this for her friends and family to keep us all healthy and energized. This is a monster dose of cruciferous veggies in one salad and it's delicious to boot!

Serves 6

ingredients

1/2 lemon, juice of

2 tbsp dijon mustard

1 tbsp shallot, chopped finely

1 clove garlic, crushed and chopped

1 1/2 tsp maple syrup

1/2 tsp pepper

1/3 cup olive oil

2 bunches kale, centre stem cut out and leaves sliced thinly

1 1/2 cups brussels sprouts, trimmed and grated or sliced thinly

1 tbsp olive oil

1/3 cup whole almonds, chopped coarsely

1 tsp sea salt

1 cup asiago or parmesan cheese, freshly grated

method

Combine lemon juice, dijon mustard, shallot, garlic, maple syrup and pepper in a small bowl.

Whisk in the olive oil.

Combine kale and brussels sprouts in a large bowl.

Heat 1 tbsp of olive oil in small saucepan and add chopped almonds and stir until golden brown.

Season almonds with sea salt and set aside to cool.

Pour dressing over kale mixture and toss to coat.

Add the grated cheese and the toasted almonds and toss again.

Serve on single plates or in a big salad bowl.

All parts of this salad can be prepared up to 8 hours ahead. Keep the chopped kale mixture and the dressing separate and covered in the fridge. Leave toasted almonds at room temperature. Toss just before serving.

spinach salad with apples and blue cheese buttermilk dressing

This combination of tart apples, blue cheese and crunchy walnuts are so reminiscent of salads served on Blvd Saint Germaine in Paris.....

Serves 6

ingredients

Dressing

2/3 cup homemade or good quality mayonnaise

2/3 cup buttermilk

1 tbsp red wine vinegar

1 clove garlic, crushed and chopped

1 tsp Worcestershire sauce

1/4 tsp cayenne

1/2 tsp salt

1/2 tsp pepper

1/3 cup blue cheese

8 cups spinach leaves

2 granny smith apples, skin on and sliced thinly

1/4 red onion, sliced thinly

1 cup walnut pieces, toasted

method

Place all dressing ingredients except blue cheese in a food processor and blend until smooth.

Add blue cheese and pulse until small pieces are still visible.

Pour into a jar and keep in the fridge. Shake well before each use.

Arrange spinach, apples, red onions and toasted walnuts on serving platter or salad bowl.

Drizzle with enough of the dressing to coat and store remainder in the fridge.

You may want to add some crispy prosciutto or bacon bits! This dressing keeps for up to two weeks in the fridge.

haricots verts and shaved fennel on spicy greens with toasted hazelnut dressing

This updated nouvelle cuisine salad is simple, light and rich at the same time. Hazelnut oil and sherry vinegar are a bit of an extravagance but you deserve it!

Serves 4

ingredients

Vinaigrette

1/2 cup hazelnuts, toasted and skinned

1/4 cup sherry vinegar

1 tsp maple syrup

1/4 tsp salt

1/4 tsp pepper

1/4 cup hazelnut oil

2 tbsp olive oil

6 cups spicy greens

1 pound haricots verts or green beans, blanched and cooled

1 cup fennel bulb, shaved or cut very thinly and drizzled with lemon juice

1 cup goat cheese, crumbled

method

Place hazelnuts in food processor, pulsing until nuts are coarsely ground.

Add sherry vinegar, maple syrup, salt and pepper and pulse until just blended.

Slowly add the hazelnut and olive oil and blend again until incorporated.

Place spicy greens on individual salad plates or on a serving platter and top with green beans, shaved fennel and crumbled goat cheese.

Drizzle the dressing over top.

You could add a grilled and sliced duck breast to turn this fabulous salad into a light dinner.

laurel's orzo and lots of spinach salad

Laurel is the queen of all things beautiful, including her love of delicious and healthy food. We love this orzo salad because of the heaping amounts of spinach. It's like a wilted spinach salad but with a bit of orzo and lots of feta. A very transportable salad that can stand up to any kind of boat, car or backpack travel!

Serves 8

ingredients

2 cups cooked orzo, about half a bag

6 cups spinach, washed

1 medium red onion, diced finely

1/2 cup kalamata olives, pitted

3 ears of fresh corn, roasted and cut off the cob in chunks (optional)

3/4 cup feta cheese, crumbled

3/4 cup pine nuts, toasted

1 whole head garlic, roasted and flesh mashed *

1/2 cup olive oil

1 tsp sea salt

1/2 tsp pepper

1/2 cup fresh basil, chopped

2 tbsp fresh dill, chopped

1/2 lemon, juice of

* see page 143

method

Cook orzo according to package instructions and place in large bowl.

Add spinach while orzo is still warm to let it wilt a bit, about 5 minutes.

Add red onion, kalamata olives, roasted corn, feta and pine nuts and toss to combine.

Combine mashed roasted garlic, olive oil, salt, pepper in a small bowl.

Add to the salad and toss well.

Add basil and dill and toss gently.

Place in a salad bowl and squeeze the lemon over top before serving.

Quinoa or Kamut are perfect wheat free substitutes for the orzo.

mango cucumber salad with mint and sweet chili vinaigrette

Another fantastic culinary creation from Annie Bailey. From years of catering and working in the food business, this girl really knows how to balance flavours and textures and when you taste this salad you will agree!

Serves 6

ingredients

Vinaigrette

1/4 cup fresh mint, chopped

1 tbsp fresh ginger, peeled and grated

1/2 tsp garlic, crushed and chopped

1/2 orange, juice and zest of

1/2 lime, juice and zest of

3 tbsp sweet chili sauce

1/4 cup rice wine vinegar

1 tsp sesame oil

1/2 cup vegetable oil

Salad

6 cups arugula or spicy greens

2 fresh mangoes, peeled and sliced thinly

1/2 red pepper, julienned

1/2 orange pepper, julienned

1/2 yellow pepper, julienned

1/4 red onion, sliced thinly

1/2 long english cucumber, halved lengthwise and sliced thinly on the diagonal

1/2 cup slivered almonds or chopped peanuts, toasted

method

Place all vinaigrette ingredients except oils in a mixing bowl and whisk to combine.

Whisk in sesame and vegetable oil slowly until well blended.

Assemble arugula or spicy greens on your favourite platter, shallow bowl or individual plates.

Top with mangoes, peppers, red onion, cucumbers and almonds.

Drizzle with vinaigrette.

Serve this salad with either the Indonesian Chicken on page 116 or the Green Curry Chicken on page 124 for a perfect summer dinner.

house salad
with clare's french vinaigrette

Everyone needs to have a simple lettuce salad in his or her repertoire, to cleanse the palate or to finish the meal. My sister Clare and her husband Basil eat this mustard infused vinaigrette with their salad almost every night of the year. They own a cozy house in France and an equally cozy one in Vancouver and this is their "house" salad.

Serves 4-6

ingredients

Vinaigrette

1 tbsp dijon mustard

1 garlic clove, crushed and chopped

1/2 cup white wine vinegar

1/2 tsp salt

1/2 tsp pepper

1 cup extra virgin olive oil

6 cups spring greens, mesclun mix or romaine lettuce

1/2 head of radicchio, ripped into bite sized pieces

1 cup sugar peas, sliced in half lengthwise

1 cup radishes, sliced thinly

1 cup oven dried cherry tomatoes (optional, see page 140 for method)

method

Place dijon mustard, garlic, vinegar, salt and pepper in a small mixing bowl and combine well.

Slowly whisk in olive oil drop by drop at first and then teaspoon-by-teaspoon until creamy and emulsified.

Arrange lettuce, radicchio, sugar peas, radishes and oven-dried tomatoes in large salad bowl.

Drizzle with vinaigrette and toss gently.

This versatile and perfectly balanced vinaigrette is fantastic with the addition of chopped fresh basil, tarragon, parsley or dill. And the combinations of lettuces and vegetables for the salad are endless. Create your own "house" salad.

lovely's incredible quinoa salad

Granted, we have quinoa salads in the previous Whitewater cookbooks but we just couldn't resist including Lovely's, my gorgeous friend from Kamloops, latest delicious version. Because, everything she makes really is lovely!

Serves 8

ingredients

2 cups multi-coloured quinoa, cooked and cooled

1 tsp salt

1/2 tsp turmeric

1 tsp paprika

1 tsp cumin

2 cups micro kale or julienned regular kale

1/2 red onion, diced finely

1 cup corn kernels, cooked and drained

1 cup red pepper, diced

1 bunch cilantro, chopped

1/2 papaya, peeled, seeded and diced

Dressing

1/2 papaya, peeled, seeded and chopped roughly

2 limes, juice of both, zest of one

1 tsp ginger, peeled and grated

4 tbsp grapeseed oil

1/4 cup liquid honey

1/4 cup fresh orange juice

1/4 tsp salt

1/4 tsp pepper

method

Combine all dressing ingredients in food processor and process until smooth. A hand-held wand blender works well too.

Toss quinoa with salt, turmeric, paprika and cumin in a large salad bowl.

Add kale, red onion, corn, red pepper, cilantro and papaya.

Pour dressing over quinoa mixture and toss gently until well combined.

Serve Lovely's Quinoa Salad with her Ancho Chilli Ribs on page 112.

tempeh salad with toasted pumpkin seed vinaigrette

This is a really good "stand alone" salad made with fermented soy called Tempeh. It is so filled with protein, veggies and seeds that we swear it will keep you going for hours!

Serves 4

ingredients

1 package plain tempeh, (or regular tofu) sliced into 1 inch strips

Marinade

2 tbsp olive oil

2 tbsp water

1/3 cup tamari

1/3 cup balsamic vinegar

1 tbsp sesame oil

1 tbsp grapeseed or vegetable oil

1 tsp pepper

1 1/2 tsp Chinese 5 spice

2 cloves garlic, crushed and chopped finely

Vinaigrette

1/2 cup pumpkin seeds, toasted

1 tbsp dijon mustard

1/2 cup apple cider vinegar

1 clove garlic, crushed

2 tsp honey

1/2 cup fresh dill, chopped

1/2 tsp salt

1/2 tsp pepper

1 cup vegetable or grape seed oil

Salad

8 cups spinach leaves

1 cup red cabbage, sliced thinly or grated

2 cups sunflower sprouts

1/2 cup pumpkin seeds, toasted, divided

4 tbsp dried cranberries

1 cup grape tomatoes, halved

1/4 long english cucumber, diced

1 cup chickpeas, drained and rinsed

2 tbsp olive oil

method

Marinade

Place tempeh strips in a shallow dish.

Whisk together all marinade ingredients.

Pour over tempeh and let marinate for 30 minutes.

Vinaigrette

Place all vinaigrette ingredients except oil in food processor and blend well.

Pour oil in gradually with food processor still running until smooth.

Salad

Combine spinach, cabbage, sprouts, pumpkin seeds, cranberries, tomatoes, cucumber and chickpeas in a large salad bowl.

Drain tempeh strips and lay on a paper towel.

Heat olive oil in sauté pan and grill tempeh strips until golden brown on both sides, about 5 minutes.

Toss salad with vinaigrette and divide onto four plates.

Top with grilled tempeh slices and garnish with extra pumpkin seeds.

This is a great portable and non-sandwich meal. An amazing addition for your your next picnic or road trip.

watermelon, mint and feta salad

This is a refreshing and mouth-watering salad for a hot summer's night on the deck. Its simplicity of flavours is a compliment to any type of grilled meat. Try it with lamb burgers and tzatziki from the *Whitewater Cooks, pure, simple and real* cookbook.

Serves 4

ingredients

5 cups watermelon, cut into 1 inch chunks

10 oz feta cheese cut into 1/2 inch cubes

1 cup fresh mint leaves, chopped

1/2 red onion, sliced thinly

1/4 cup extra virgin olive oil

1 tsp maldon or sea salt

1/2 tsp pepper

method

Place the watermelon chunks in the bottom of a shallow bowl or on a platter.

Sprinkle the feta and mint over the watermelon.

Add a layer of onions.

Try some fresh basil instead of mint. Keep it simple!

Drizzle with olive oil.

Season with salt and pepper.

seared scallop and crispy prosciutto salad with passion fruit vinaigrette

My kids and I created this beautiful salad on one of our holidays in Maui. We think this combination is just about the best summertime lunch you could ever dream of and it is also a decadent starter to any dinner! Pomegranates are a delicious substitute if papayas can't be found.

Serves 4

ingredients

Vinaigrette

2 tbsp apple cider vinegar

3 tbsp passion fruit jelly or jam*

1/2 tsp salt

1/2 tsp pepper

1 tbsp fresh basil, chopped

1 tsp ginger, peeled, grated and chopped finely

1/2 cup oil

2 heads butter lettuce, washed and torn into bite size pieces

1 papaya, diced

1 package (125 g) prosciutto, in whole pieces on a baking tray in oven for 12-15 minutes at 375°F, until crisp.

1/2 cup macadamia nuts, chopped

1 avocado, diced

2 – 3 tbsp butter

20 large scallops, fresh if possible or frozen and thawed

method

Place apple cider vinegar, passion fruit jelly, salt, pepper, basil and ginger in small mixing bowl and whisk until blended.

Whisk in oil until well combined.

Arrange lettuce, papaya, crispy prosciutto pieces, macadamia nuts and avocado on individual salad plates.

Heat butter in large frying pan on medium high heat until

just starting to brown.

Add scallops and fry on each side for about 3 minutes, until golden brown and just cooked.

Arrange 5 scallops on each salad plate and drizzle with vinaigrette.

*passion fruit or lilikoi jelly can be found in Culinary Conspiracy or most specialty food stores.

If you happen to be in Hawaii or anywhere that sells fresh Lillikoi fruit, add a whole one to the dressing, unbelievable!

dinners

mushroom nut loaf with miso gravy

If you are craving comfort food, this is for you! It tastes just like Sunday night dinner and when accompanied with our Miso Gravy on page 136 and mashed yams or potatoes, you will heave a sigh of happiness! My daughter Ali Adams is a very healthy eater and shared this fabulous recipe with us for all you vegans out there!

Serves 4

ingredients

2 cups onions, diced finely

4 tbsp olive oil

4 garlic cloves, crushed and chopped

4 cups mushrooms, chopped coarsely in a food processor

1 1/2 cups raw cashews, soaked in water for at least 15 minutes, drained and chopped coarsely in a food processor

2 cup walnuts, chopped coarsely in food processor

2 tbsp cornstarch

2 lemons , juice of

1 cup marsala wine or sherry

1/2 cup rice flour

1 tsp fresh or dried rosemary, chopped finely

1 tsp fresh or dried thyme, chopped finely

1/2 tsp dried tarragon

1/2 tsp fresh or dried, sage, chopped finely

1 tsp salt

1 tsp pepper

method

Preheat oven to 350°F.

Sauté onions on medium – low heat in olive oil until soft, about 5 minutes.

Add garlic, mushrooms, cashews and walnuts.

Cook until dry and liquid has reduced, about 10 minutes.

Combine cornstarch, lemon juice, marsala, flour and all spices and blend until smooth.

Add to mushroom mixture and cook for another 5-10 minutes, until absorbed and thick.

Press into a greased loaf pan.

Bake for 30 minutes.

Serve right out of the loaf pan or flip it out onto a platter and slice.

To complete this healthy dinner include our Kale Caesar Salad on page 70.

crispy pork belly with quince sauce and creamy cinnamon yams

The total crispiness of the pork skin and the tartness of the quince sauce are a winning combination and once in awhile we really need to treat our taste buds! You just need to eat a LITTLE slice of the pork belly and LOTS of yams and quince sauce.

Serves 4

ingredients

4 medium sized yams, peeled and cut in chunks

1 tbsp olive oil

1/2 tsp cinnamon

1/2 tsp ground ginger

sea salt

freshly ground black pepper

2 1/2 -3 lb pork belly*

1 tbsp sea salt

1 tbsp Chinese five spice powder

1 tbsp olive oil

1/2 cup quince paste, chopped**

1/4 cup brown sugar

1/4 cup apple cider vinegar

1/2 cup chicken stock

1/4 cup port

method

Preheat oven to 400°F.

Toss yams with olive oil, cinnamon, ginger, salt and pepper.

Place on a baking sheet and roast for 45 minutes or until golden and tender.

Place in a food processor and process until smooth, set aside and keep warm. You will probably need to reheat them before serving.

Turn oven down to 350°F.

Score the pork skin on the pork belly at one inch intervals.

Combine salt and Chinese five spice and rub it all over the pork.

Rub the remaining olive oil on the skin of the pork belly.

Place pork, skin side down on a baking pan and roast for 2 1/2 hours.

Increase oven temperature to 425°F and turn the pork over and roast for another 1/2 hour until the skin is golden and crispy.

While pork is cooking, make the quince sauce.

Place the quince paste, brown sugar, vinegar, chicken stock and port in a small saucepan over medium heat and cook, stirring occasionally for about 3 minutes until the quince paste has dissolved.

Increase heat to high and let sauce boil for another 4-5 minutes until it has thickened slightly.

*available at Railway Station Meats and Deli

**available at Culinary Conspiracy

To serve, divide pureed yams onto 4 plates or a serving platter, top with slices of pork belly and drizzle with quince sauce.

butternut squash and rapini lasagne

This is a vegetarian twist on an old favourite. Rapini is a vegetable commonly used in southern Italian cuisine and is full of all things that are good for us!

Serves 6-8

ingredients

Filling

4 lbs butternut squash, peeled, seeded and cut crosswise into 1/4 inch slices

1 tsp salt

1 tsp pepper

3 tbsp olive oil

2 lbs rapini, tough stems removed

1/2 tsp red pepper flakes

2 cups mozzarella, grated

1 lb (475 g) ricotta cheese

1 3/4 cups parmesan, grated

1 lemon, zest of

2 tsp fresh sage, chopped finely

1 tsp fresh rosemary, chopped finely

12 lasagne noodles

3/4 cup parmesan, grated

Béchamel Sauce

1/4 cup butter

1/4 cup flour

5 cups milk

1/4 tsp nutmeg

1 bay leaf

1/2 tsp salt

1/2 tsp pepper

method

Filling

Preheat oven to 350°F.

Place squash, salt, pepper and olive oil in a large bowl.

Toss to coat evenly.

Place on two baking sheets and roast until tender, about 20-25 minutes and let cool.

Blanch rapini in boiling water for 1 minute, until just wilted.

Drain and cool, squeezing out excess water.

Chop rapini coarsely, transfer to a medium bowl, toss with red pepper flakes and salt and pepper.

Mix mozzarella, ricotta, 1 cup parmesan, lemon zest, sage and rosemary in a small bowl and set aside.

Cook lasagne noodles as per package instructions, rinse, drain and set aside.

Béchamel Sauce

Melt butter in a large saucepan over medium heat.

Add flour and stir until combined for about 2 minutes, to make a roux.

Add milk gradually, whisking to blend into a smooth sauce.

Whisk continuously and let thicken, about 8 minutes.

Add nutmeg, bay leaf, salt and pepper and turn to low heat and cook for another minute or two to combine flavours.

This lasagne is great with the usual classics, a crisp green salad and baked garlic baguette!
If you can't find rapini, which is also called broccoli rabe, try substituting with kale, gai lan or spinach.

Preheat oven to 375°F.

Ladle 1/4 cup béchamel sauce into greased 9 x 13 inch baking dish and spread evenly over bottom.

Line dish with a single layer of lasagne noodles.

Layer 1/3 of the squash on top, then 1/3 of the rapini.

Sprinkle 1/3 of reserved cheese mixture on veggies.

Spoon 1/3 cup béchamel sauce over cheese.

Repeat procedure 2 more times for a 3 layer lasagne, finishing with béchamel.

Sprinkle remaining 3/4 cup parmesan over entire dish.

Bake for 45 minutes or until lasagne starts to bubble.

Broil for 4 – 6 minutes until golden brown on top.

Remove from oven, cover and let rest for 20 minutes before serving.

beef tenderloin with chimichurri sauce

Margie is a treasured friend and the most energetic and interesting person we have ever met. She always has the best recipes for uncomplicated entertaining and she often has a crowd of adult "kids" for dinner on Sunday night. She will fling together a big yummy feast for those that show up hungry and in need of a stand-in mother!

Serves 6

ingredients

one 3-4 lb beef tenderloin

Chimichurri Sauce

3/4 cup olive oil

3 tbsp red wine vinegar

1 lemon, juice of

3 garlic cloves, peeled

3 shallots, peeled

1 tsp salt

1/2 tsp pepper

1/2 tsp red chili flakes

3 cups parsley, stems removed

2 cups cilantro, stems removed

1 cup fresh mint, stems removed

Spice Rub

2 tbsp brown sugar

1 tbsp sweet smoked paprika

1 tbsp coarse salt

1 1/2 tsp ancho chili powder

1 tsp black pepper, freshly ground

method

Remove tenderloin from fridge and let sit at room temperature, about 1 hour.

Place olive oil, vinegar, lemon juice, garlic, shallots, salt, pepper and chili flakes in a food processor and pulse until chopped and blended.

Add handfuls of herbs (parsley, cilantro, mint) with processor running and blend until smooth.

Transfer to a deep bowl and set aside.

Preheat barbeque to medium - high heat.

Combine spice rub ingredients in a bowl and mix well.

Pat tenderloin dry and rub with olive oil and sprinkle all over with spice rub.

Sear tenderloin for 2 minutes on all sides.

Reduce heat to medium and grill uncovered until meat is 130°F or about 25 minutes for medium rare.

Remove from grill and let rest on a serving platter covered in tin foil for at least 15- 20 minutes before slicing.

Serve with the Chimichuri Sauce on the side.

Margie recommends serving the Chimichurri Sauce with salmon and prawns as well!
Polenta eggplant parmesan on page 114 completes this dinner.

drunken prawns

This is the very, very talented Annie Bailey's signature dish and people travel miles to have their taste buds dazzled by her cuisine, especially by these addictive prawns. Annie has been in the food business for many years and her energy is boundless!

Serves 4

ingredients

4-6 cups cooked basmati or jasmine rice

Drunken Sauce

1/2 medium onion, diced finely

2 tbsp garlic, crushed and chopped

4 tbsp galangal root, peeled and grated*

1 tbsp vegetable oil

1/4 cup Jack Daniel's bourbon

1 cup teriyaki sauce

1/2 cup sweet chili sauce

1 tsp chili paste (sambal oelek)

1/4 cup oyster sauce

1/4 cup ketchup

10 lime leaves, fresh if available

1 lemongrass stalk, cut into 3 pieces, bruised

1/2 cup Thai basil, julienned

Prawns & Vegetables

2 tbsp vegetable oil

1 lb of prawns (about 24 prawns), raw and peeled, tails on

1/4 red pepper, julienned

1/4 orange pepper, julienned

1/4 yellow pepper, julienned

4 green onions, sliced into 1 inch lengths

method

Sauté onion, garlic and galangal in oil until softened, about 4 minutes.

Add Jack Daniel's and stir for approximately 2 minutes to deglaze pan.

Add teriyaki sauce, sweet chili sauce, sambal oelek, oyster sauce, ketchup, lime leaves and lemongrass.

Simmer on low heat for 15 minutes, stirring occasionally.

Remove lime leaves and lemongrass.

Add Thai basil.

Heat a wok or large frying pan and add 2 tbsp vegetable oil and sauté prawns until just turning pink.

Add peppers and green onions and sauté for a few seconds.

Add the drunken sauce and simmer until the prawns are cooked through, about 3 more minutes.

Serve over basmati or jasmine rice.

*available at Ellison's and most specialty food stores.

If you like a spicier sauce, just increase the amount of chili paste.

lamb chops with cashew mint pesto

This totally flavourful pesto can swing both ways. It is so good on lamb chops and it is also wonderful when tossed with zucchini ribbons or pasta to make a simple vegetarian dish.

Serves 4

ingredients

8 - 12 lamb chops

Pesto

1 cup fresh mint, de-stemmed

1 cup fresh parsley, de-stemmed

1 cup unsalted cashew pieces, soaked in water for a minimum of 15 minutes and drained

2 garlic cloves, skins off and chopped coarsely

1/2 cup nutritional yeast flakes

2 tbsp tamari or soy sauce

1 tbsp apple cider vinegar

1 tbsp maple syrup

method

Combine all pesto ingredients in food processor and blend until smooth, making sure to scrape down the edges a few times.

Preheat oven to 400°F.

Place lamb chops on a baking sheet and spread the top side with pesto.

Cook in top third of oven for 15-20 minutes, for medium rare chops.

To make zucchini ribbons, peel zucchinis with a peeler into single, long strips, rotating around the zucchini until you are left with only the very seedy center. Place them in a bowl and toss with the Cashew Mint Pesto.

fennel sausage risotto

Make this flavourful risotto for a comforting and cozy little dinner. The combination of the fennel, tomatoes and parmesan and the spiciness of the sausages are just so perfect. A simple arugula salad, a crusty baguette, with a side dish of olive oil, sea salt and balsamic vinegar and your life, at that moment, is complete!

Serves 6

ingredients

6 cups low sodium chicken or vegetable stock, heated

1 cup white wine

1/4 cup butter

1 lb (about 6) hot or medium Italian sausages, squeezed out of casings

1 medium onion, finely diced

2 cloves garlic, crushed and chopped

2/3 cup fresh tomatoes, diced

1 tbsp fennel seeds

1 tbsp fresh thyme or basil, chopped finely

2 cups Arborio rice

1 tsp sea salt

1/2 tsp pepper

1 cup parmesan cheese, grated

1/2 cup fresh tomatoes, diced finely

1/2 cup parsley, chopped

method

Bring stock and wine to a boil, reduce heat and keep at a gentle simmer.

Melt half the butter in a large, heavy-bottomed pot.

Add the sausage meat, separating it with a wooden spoon into quarter-sized pieces, while it cooks over medium heat for 3 - 4 minutes.

Add onion and garlic and cook another 10 minutes.

Add tomatoes, fennel seeds and thyme (or basil) and simmer for 5 minutes.

Stir in the rice and cook for about a minute or two, until the rice is heated slightly.

Add the hot stock and wine, one ladle at a time, stirring gently with a wooden spoon until all the liquid is absorbed before adding more.

Keep the risotto at a lively simmer, adding a ladle of stock at a time to keep it moist.

Continue until most or all of the stock is used and the rice is tender and creamy, about 25 -30 minutes.

Season with sea salt and pepper.

Stir in the remaining butter and the parmesan.

Add a bit more hot stock just before serving if risotto has become too firm.

Garnish with diced tomatoes and chopped parsley.

Folding in some fresh arugula is a really nice addition to this risotto.

havana chicken

This Cuban inspired overnight marinade, butterflied and flattened grilling technique is the secret to the depth of flavour that makes this dish sing. Cooked in a cast iron grill pan on the barbeque for the very best effect, the skin is caramelized and the chicken is moist.

Serves 4

ingredients

1 - 3lb whole organic chicken

1 lemon, sliced thinly

2 lemons, juice and zest of

1/4 cup olive oil

2 tbsp dried oregano

2 tbsp smoked paprika

1 1/2 tsp cumin

2 tsp allspice

10 cloves garlic, crushed

1 tsp salt

1/2 tsp pepper

1 lemon, halved

1/2 cup cilantro, chopped

method

Place the chicken, breast side down, on a cutting board so the back is facing you. Using a sharp knife or kitchen scissors, cut through the ribs on one side of the backbone.

Lay chicken open, cut through the ribs on the other side of the backbone and remove and discard the backbone.

Flip chicken over and crack the breastbone by pressing down with the flat side of the knife until the chicken lays flat.

Place butterflied chicken, breast side up, in a shallow baking dish.

Loosen chicken skin from thighs and breast with your fingers and slide lemon slices under skin.

Place lemon juice and zest, olive oil, oregano, paprika, cumin, allspice, garlic, salt and pepper in food processor and pulse into a paste.

Rub paste all over chicken.

Cover and marinate in fridge overnight.

Preheat barbeque to medium - high heat.

Wrap a brick, flat rock or the lid of a cast iron lid with tin foil.

Preheat both the brick and the cast iron pan in the barbeque for about 5 minutes.

Brush hot pan with olive oil.

Place chicken, breast side down, into hot pan and lay wrapped brick on top of meat.

Close barbeque and turn down to medium heat.

Grill chicken for 30 minutes and then flip over, lifting carefully and slowly to keep the skin on the chicken.

Remove brick and cook a further 20 minutes or until juices from the chicken run clear when pricked with a skewer.

Turn barbeque off, leaving chicken inside for 10 more minutes to rest.

Transfer to serving platter and surround with grilled fresh lemon halves and cilantro.

Roasting this chicken, brick included, in the oven is a good alternative and with the same delectable results. The chicken sandwiches the next day are to die for!

jambalaya

Every culture has its "family" dish and this Cajun version of Jambalaya is full of smoky, salty, sweet and delicious flavours. If you are pining for the Bayou then a heaping plate of this will fix you right up!

Serves 6-8

ingredients

2 cups short grain brown rice, uncooked

5 mild Italian sausages, sliced into 2 inch pieces

3 smoked farmer's sausages, sliced into 2 inch pieces

3/4 lb smoked ham, diced into 1/2 inch pieces (optional)

2 lbs prawns, with shells on or off

1 medium onion, diced

2 cloves garlic, crushed and chopped

2 sticks celery, chopped finely

1 red pepper, diced

2 cups peas, fresh or frozen

1 cup barbeque sauce, store bought or Gussy's barbeque sauce found on page 155

1 tsp smoked paprika

1/2 tsp liquid smoke

1 tsp salt

1/2 tsp black pepper

1/4 tsp red chili flakes (or more if you like it hot)

1/2 tsp thyme

method

Prepare rice according to package instructions.

Sauté both sausages and ham until browned and crispy, about 8 – 10 minutes and transfer into a large bowl and add the prawns.

Sauté onion, garlic, celery and red pepper until just tender in the same pan that was used for the sausages and ham, about 5 minutes.

Add onion mixture and peas to bowl with the sausages, ham and prawns.

Preheat oven to 350°F.

Grease a 9 x 13 inch ovenproof casserole dish.

Whisk together 1/2 cup of the barbeque sauce, smoked paprika, liquid smoke, salt and pepper, chili flakes and thyme.

Pour over sausage and prawn mixture and stir well.

Stir the remaining barbeque sauce into the cooled rice and place into the casserole dish.

Spread sausage and prawn mix over the rice, cover with lid or foil and bake for 40 minutes or until hot.

Fill your house with delicious aromas and invite a big gang over for dinner!

ancho chili ribs with smoky apple barbeque sauce

Our friend Lovely, went to Costa Rica where she tasted some delicious ribs that she just loved.   When she came home, she recreated them and made them even better! She now officially calls herself the " Rib Meister".

Serves 4

ingredients

2 racks of baby back ribs

Rub

1 tbsp ancho chili powder

1/4 cup paprika

2 tbsp dry mustard

3 tbsp brown sugar

2 tbsp coarse salt

2 tbsp cumin

2 tbsp garlic powder

1 tsp pepper

Barbeque Sauce

3 apples, peeled and chopped finely

1 large onion, diced

3 cloves garlic, crushed

1 tsp fresh ginger, peeled and grated

1 tsp oil

1 tsp cumin

1/2 tsp cinnamon

1 tbsp chipotle chilies in adobe sauce, chopped finely

1 cup apple juice

1/2 cup ketchup

1/2 cup honey

1 cup brown sugar

2 tbsp Worcestershire sauce

1/2 tsp liquid smoke

1 tbsp cornstarch mixed with 1/2 cup apple cider vinegar

method

Combine ancho chili powder, paprika, dry mustard, brown sugar, salt, cumin, garlic powder and pepper in a small bowl.

Rub ribs on both sides with the rub mixture, keep the remainder in your spice cupboard.

Wrap each rack with tin foil and refrigerate overnight.

Preheat oven to 325°F.

Open each package and drizzle with a bit of apple juice and rewrap.

Bake until tender, about 1 1/2 hours.

Make the barbeque sauce.

Sauté apples, onion, garlic and ginger in oil in a heavy bottomed pot for about 10 minutes until apples and onions are soft.

Add the cumin, cinnamon and chipotle chilies and sauté for another few seconds.

Add apple juice, ketchup, honey, sugar, Worcestershire sauce and liquid smoke.

Simmer until thickened, about 15 minutes.

Blend with a hand-held mixing wand until smooth.

Add the cornstarch and apple cider vinegar mixture and simmer until thickened, about 2 minutes.

Remove ribs from oven, take them out of the tin foil and drain excess fat.

Brush liberally with barbeque sauce and bake or barbeque for a further 20-30 minutes.

Linda says to make a batch of this in the fall when the apples are bountiful!

polenta eggplant parmesan

This is a fabulous vegetarian, wheat free dinner all on its own or an accompaniment to your favorite meat or fish.

Serves 8-10

ingredients

Polenta

4 cups water

1 tsp salt

1 cup cornmeal

1/2 cup sun dried tomatoes, chopped

1/2 cup fresh basil, chopped

2 tbsp fresh rosemary, chopped finely

1/2 cup goat cheese, crumbled

2-3 large fresh mozzarella balls, sliced or 2 cups regular mozzarella, grated and divided

1 large eggplant, sliced and grilled*

4 small to medium zucchinis, sliced and grilled*

2 cups good quality tomato sauce, homemade or store bought

3/4 cup parmesan cheese, grated

method

Bring water to a boil and add salt.

Whisk in corn meal slowly to prevent lumps.

Switch to a wooden spoon and keep stirring on medium low heat for 8 minutes until thickened.

Remove from heat and stir in sun dried tomatoes, basil, rosemary and goat cheese.

Grease a 10 inch oval or rectangular baking dish.

Spread polenta in bottom of the dish.

Place a layer of mozzarella on polenta.

Place the eggplant and zucchini slices on top of the mozzarella.

Pour tomato sauce over to cover.

Sprinkle with parmesan.

Top with remaining mozzarella.

Bake at 350°F for 40-50 minutes.

*to grill vegetables, toss the slices with a bit of olive oil and salt and pepper and place on a preheated barbecue and grill for about 3 minutes per side or until grill marks appear and vegetables feel soft. You can also bake them in the oven at 350 °F for 15-20 minutes.

Feel free to use other vegetables of your liking. We have added mushrooms, red peppers and fennel with wonderful results!

indonesian chicken

If you want to whip something together quickly and need more than a stir-fry or your favourite go-to weeknight dinner then this is it. Really tasty and super fast to throw together, ingredients are something you probably have in your fridge anyway! If not, make sure they are!

Serves 4

ingredients

2 medium onions, diced

3 cloves garlic, crushed and chopped

3 tbsp olive oil

8 - 10 boneless chicken breasts or thighs, cut into 1/2 inch strips

1 cup low sodium chicken stock

3 tbsp white vinegar

1/2 cup kecap manis*

3 tbsp ketchup

2 tbsp brown sugar

1 tbsp sambal oelek**

2 tbsp tamarind paste mixed with 1/2 cup hot water and pressed through a sieve (optional)

6 tbsp peanut butter, unsweetened

1 cup bean sprouts

1/2 cup cilantro, chopped

1/2 cup peanuts, roasted and chopped

2 limes, quartered

method

Sauté onions and garlic in olive oil in a heavy-bottomed saucepan until softened – about 5 minutes.

Add chicken strips, stir well and let brown and cook for 10 minutes.

Combine chicken stock, vinegar, kecap manis, ketchup, brown sugar, sambal oelek, tamarind water and peanut butter in a bowl and mix well.

Add to chicken and cook on medium heat until chicken is cooked, another 10-15 minutes.

Serve topped with fresh bean sprouts, chopped cilantro, peanuts and a squeeze of lime.

*kecap manis is a sweet, thick soy sauce originating in Indonesia, available at Ellison's Market and most grocery stores.

**sambal oelek is red chili paste. It is available in most grocery stores.

Great served on a bed of basmati rice or rice noodles. If you are looking for a vegetarian dish with peanutty flavours substitute the chicken with tofu strips and add some fresh spinach.

pan seared sablefish with caper, tomato and dill beurre blanc sauce

We love fish and there are never too many preparations. Sablefish is also known as black cod and is one of the most flavourful and rich fishes to swim the seas.   Seared quickly in a hot pan, finished in the oven and topped with a beurre blanc sauce. Yum!

Serves 4

ingredients

Beurre Blanc Sauce

2 shallots, diced finely

3/4 cup white wine

2 tbsp white wine vinegar

1/2 cup butter, cold and cut in little cubes

1 tbsp fresh dill, chopped

4 – 6 ounce pieces of sablefish

1 tbsp olive oil

1 tsp salt

1/2 tsp pepper

1/4 cup capers or caper berries

1 cup acorn or cherry tomatoes, halved

1/2 cup kalamata olives, pitted and halved (optional)

method

Place shallots, wine and vinegar in a small saucepan and simmer until reduced by half, about 15 minutes.

Add butter gradually whisking well after each addition until completely incorporated into sauce.

Stir in the dill and keep sauce on very low heat while you cook the fish.

Preheat oven to 375°F.

Brush fish with olive oil and sprinkle with salt and pepper.

Sear fish in a large ovenproof sauté pan on medium high heat for about 2 minutes per side.

Add capers, tomatoes and olives and place pan in oven and cook for 8-10 minutes or until fish is just cooked.

Place fish on serving plates, top with the capers, tomatoes and olives from the sauté pan and drizzle with beurre blanc sauce.

We like to serve this fish with mashed celery root and potatoes.

pat's sunday night pasta

Another truly Italian pasta dish from the "husband-we-all-wish-we-had-in-our-kitchens," Pat McLaughlin. It is a beautiful one pot family dinner that has something in it for everyone.

Serves 8-10

ingredients

3 tbsp extra virgin olive oil

3 - 4 garlic cloves, crushed and chopped

1 tbsp dried oregano

1 cup fresh basil, chopped

8-10 Italian sausages, hot or medium

2 jars (650 ml each) of your favourite tomato pasta sauce

method

Heat olive oil in a large frying pan on medium heat and add garlic, oregano and basil and heat for 1 minute.

Add sausages and cook with a spatter guard on until the sausages are almost cooked through, about 5 minutes per side, moving them a few times.

Add pasta sauce and cook on low heat for 30 minutes, stirring often.

Remove sausages from pan, cool and cut into thirds and place sausages in two 9x13 inch glass baking dishes or one large ovenproof baking pan.

ingredients

Filling for pasta shells

2 medium chicken breasts, broiled until cooked and shredded into 1/2 inch pieces

2 cups ricotta cheese

1 cup mozzarella, grated

1/2 cup parmesan, grated

2 cups spinach, blanched, cooled and chopped finely

1 tbsp parsley, chopped

2 tbsp fresh basil, chopped

1 tsp salt

1/2 tsp pepper

1 box large pasta shells (340 g)

1 cup mozzarella, grated

1/2 cup parmesan, grated

method

Place all filling ingredients in a large bowl and combine well.

Bring salted water to a boil and cook shells until just al dente, do not over cook.

Drain pasta and rinse with cold running water while in the colander. This "shocks" the pasta and stops it from cooking any longer and makes the shells easier to stuff.

Stuff each shell generously with the filling mixture.

Place the shells in the baking dishes with the sausages.

Ladle pasta sauce over shells and sausages, saving some of the pasta sauce to be served at the table.

Sprinkle with the mozzarella and parmesan and cover with tin foil.

Bake for 20 minutes at 400°F.

Serve at the table right out of the baking dishes.

A classic Italian green salad and a fresh baguette or focaccia completes Pat's Sunday Night Pasta dish!!

mediterranean lamb shanks

This amazing dish is similar to the classic osso buco but we are using lamb shanks instead of veal. This is rich in mediterranean flavour and we like to serve it with roasted garlic mashed potatoes.

Serves 6

ingredients

6 lamb shanks

4 tbsp olive oil

1/4 cup flour

1/2 tsp salt

1/2 tsp pepper

1 large onion, diced

3 stalks celery, diced

3 large carrots, peeled and diced

3 cloves garlic, crushed

1 1/2 cups white wine

1 1/2 cups beef broth

2 - 28 oz cans diced tomatoes, with liquid

3 sprigs fresh thyme, chopped finely or 1 tsp dried

3 sprigs fresh oregano, chopped finely or 1 tsp dried

1/4 cup fresh rosemary, chopped finely or 1 tbsp dried

2 bay leaves

1 cup kalamata olives, pitted and halved

1 1/2 cups fresh parsley, chopped

1/2 cup fresh mint, chopped

2 cloves garlic, crushed and chopped

2 tbsp lemon zest

1/2 cup pine nuts, toasted

fresh mint and parsley for garnish

method

Preheat oven to 325°F.

Heat olive oil over medium high heat in a large, heavy-bottomed ovenproof pot.

Toss lamb shanks in flour mixed with the salt and pepper, until lightly coated.

Sear shanks on all sides until browned. You may have to do this in two batches.

Remove shanks and set aside.

Reduce heat to medium and add onion, celery, carrots, garlic and sauté for 5 minutes.

Stir in wine, beef broth, tomatoes, thyme, oregano, rosemary and bay leaves.

Add shanks back into pot, making sure they are almost covered with sauce. Add more beef broth or wine if necessary.

Bring to a simmer, cover and place in oven for at least 2 1/2 hours.

Stir in kalamata olives after 2 hours of cooking and return to oven for the last 30 minutes.

Remove from oven and add parsley, mint, garlic, lemon zest and pine nuts and stir into sauce just before serving.

Garnish with chopped mint and parsley.

If you have left over sauce, add some cubed lamb shoulder which creates a delicious dinner for another night!

emmy's hungarian beef goulash

Emmy is our dear friend who loves dressing up more than anyone we know! She has picked up her husband Blake, at the airport, wearing a full pig's costume just for fun! This is the dish we always make for Halloween because it fills up the little trick-or-treaters before they head out. It is fun because we refer to it as "Ghoul-ash" and the kids go wild, thinking that there may be ghosts in the stew!

Serves 10

ingredients

5 lbs stewing beef or chuck roast, cut into 1 inch cubes

1/4 cup butter

1/4 cup olive oil

1 tsp sea salt

1/2 tsp ground pepper

5 lbs yellow onions, diced

1/4 cup hungarian paprika

3 cups beef stock

1 cup sour cream

1/2 cup parsley for garnish

method

Heat 1 tbsp butter and 1 tbsp oil in large, heavy-bottomed saucepan over medium high heat.

Cook beef in batches, allowing the meat to become well browned on all sides, about 3-5 minutes.

Season each batch with salt and pepper.

Set meat aside in a separate bowl.

Reduce heat to low and using same pan, add remaining butter, oil and onions.

Cook onions until translucent, about 15 minutes.

Return beef to pot and add paprika and stock.

Stir well to combine and continue simmering on very low heat for 1 1/2 - 2 hours, stirring occasionally.

Serve with mashed potatoes or egg noodles and a dollop of sour cream and chopped parsley. This is the easiest recipe, which is perfect for an evening of no fiddling in the kitchen, leaving lots of time for pumpkin carving. A platter of fresh crudités with a few dips and you are set.

tuscan beef involtini
with pancetta and parmigiano

Classic Italian flavours blend in this hearty beef dish. Best eaten on a bed of gnocchi and some steamed kale and with a glass of hearty Chianti at your elbow. Blink and you'll think you're in Nona's kitchen!

Serves 6

ingredients

6 beef rouladen*

1/2 cup flat leaf parsley

1/2 cup fresh basil leaves

1/2 medium onion, diced

2 cloves garlic, peeled

3 tbsp olive oil

1 tsp salt

1 tsp pepper

4 oz pancetta, sliced very thinly

1/2 lb piece of Parmigiano Reggiano cheese

1/2 cup flour

1 tbsp butter

3/4 cup red wine

*Rouladen cuts can be found in the meat department of most grocery stores.

method

Unroll rouladen slices and lay flat on a cutting board.

Pulse parsley, basil, onion, garlic and olive oil in food processor until you have a coarse paste.

Divide paste evenly onto all 6 pieces of rouladen, so you have about a 1/4 inch layer on each piece.

Sprinkle with salt and pepper.

Lay a thin layer of pancetta on each meat slice.

Slice Parmigiano with cheese slicer so you have enough slices to cover the meat with a single layer.
Place cheese on pancetta.

Roll each filled meat slice, starting from the skinny end, tucking sides as you roll.

Tie with string or pierce with a toothpick to secure the roll.

Place flour on shallow plate and roll each meat roll until well coated.

Melt butter in a heavy bottomed saucepan that is large enough to hold all the rolls.

Brown the rolls evenly on all sides about 5 to 8 minutes.

Add wine, reduce heat to simmer, cover and cook until tender, about 10 minutes.

You can prepare the involtini in advance and just leave the cooking part until the end.

green curry chicken with roasted eggplant and red peppers

Another really easy dinner idea. We make this aromatic curry with chicken thighs and bake it in the oven for a simple preparation with outstanding results.

Serves 4

ingredients

1/2 cup green curry paste *

1 - 400 ml can coconut milk

2 tbsp fish sauce

1 tbsp sugar

6 kaffir lime leaves**

1 stalk lemongrass, cut in thirds, bruised

8 chicken thighs, bone in, skin on

1 tsp salt

1 Japanese or regular eggplant, diced

1 red pepper, diced

2 tbsp olive oil

1 cup mini cucumbers, sliced thinly

1 cup micro-herbs or cilantro, chopped

1 lime, juice of

*use your favourite green curry paste, we like Thai Kitchen
** available at Ellison's Market

method

Preheat oven to 350°F.

Place curry paste, coconut milk, fish sauce, sugar, lime leaves and lemongrass in ovenproof baking dish and combine well.

Rub the chicken with salt and place, skin side up, in baking dish.

Cover with lid or tin foil and bake for 1 hour.

Remove foil from chicken dish and bake for another 30 minutes until chicken is cooked and skin is brown and crispy.

Toss eggplant and peppers with olive oil and place on a separate baking sheet.

Roast the eggplant and red peppers on the separate baking sheet in the oven for the final 30 minutes with the chicken.

Arrange cooked eggplant and peppers around chicken thighs in the baking dish and garnish with cucumbers and micro-herbs.

Squeeze lime juice over the complete dish.

Serve this Green Curry Chicken with basmati rice that has been tossed with toasted cashews, sesame seeds and coconut flakes, you will feel transported by the flavours of Thailand.

tourtière with homemade ketchup

This hearty meat pie is a classic Québécois tradition and can be traced back to the 17th century. We love to eat it after a chilly day of skiing and of course on Christmas Eve! Serve with the delicious homemade ketchup, which can be found on the following page.

Serves 6

ingredients

2 unbaked 8 inch pastry shells* (one is for the top crust)

2 tbsp butter

1 medium onion, diced

3 cloves garlic, crushed and chopped

1 celery stalk, diced finely

1 lb lean ground beef

1 lb lean ground pork

1/2 cup white wine

1 tsp salt

1 tsp fresh ground pepper

1/2 tsp cinnamon

1/2 tsp savory

1/2 tsp cloves

1/2 tsp nutmeg

1 baking potato, peeled, cooked and mashed

1 egg mixed with 2 tsp water (egg wash)

method

Melt butter over medium heat in large saucepan.

Add onion, garlic and celery and sauté until soft, about 5 minutes.

Add beef and pork and sauté for another 8 minutes, stirring often.

Pour wine into mixture, reduce heat to low, cover and simmer for 30 minutes.

Add salt, pepper, cinnamon, savory, cloves, nutmeg and mashed potato and combine well.

Simmer uncovered for another 5 minutes.

Remove from heat, transfer to another bowl and let cool for 30 minutes.

Preheat oven to 425°F.

Place frozen pie crust on parchment lined baking tray.

Spoon cooled ground meat filling into pie shell and pack down gently.

Brush pastry edge with some of the egg wash.

Place the second pastry shell on top of the pork mixture.

Crimp to seal edges together.

Brush the top and edge of pie with egg wash.

Cut a few vents in top to let steam out.

Bake for 15 minutes, reduce heat to 375°F and bake until golden brown, about 40 minutes.

Remove from oven and let rest on cooling rack for 15 minutes before cutting and serving.

Pre-made pie shells can be purchased at most grocery stores or make our Perfect Pie Crust from Whitewater Cooks with Friends.

homemade ketchup

This recipe makes enough ketchup to replace the store-bought one in your fridge. And you will love this homemade version because it is so much better!

Makes 4 Cups

ingredients

12 roma tomatoes, diced

2 carrots, peeled and diced

1 onion, diced

4 cloves garlic, crushed and chopped

1 red pepper, diced

2 apples, peeled and cored, cut into chunks

1 tbsp vegetable oil

1 tsp salt

1/2 tsp fresh ground pepper

3/4 tsp allspice

1 can (5.5 oz) tomato paste

1/2 cup apple cider vinegar

1/2 cup brown sugar

1 cup water

method

Preheat oven to 375°F.

Toss tomatoes, carrots, onion, garlic, red pepper and apples in the vegetable oil and spread onto two baking sheets and roast until tender, about 45 minutes.

Remove from oven and purée in a food processor until smooth.

Strain purée through a sieve into a large saucepan.

Keeps up to one month in the fridge.

Add salt, pepper, allspice, tomato paste, vinegar, brown sugar and water and bring to a boil.

Reduce heat to a simmer until sauce has the consistency of ketchup, about 20 minutes.

Cool completely and transfer to a glass jar with a tight fitting lid.

red snapper with tamarind sauce

Such a lovely fresh sauce and an easy preparation for red snapper which is a gorgeous, affordable and readily available fish. This sauce is also great for prawns and any white fish.

Serves 2

ingredients

2 tbsp tamarind, from a block*

1 cup cold water

2 shallots, sliced thinly

3 garlic cloves, crushed and chopped

1 tbsp fresh cilantro, stems only, chopped finely

1 tbsp fish sauce

1 1/2 tsp sugar

1/4 tsp salt

2 green onions, sliced diagonally

1 medium sized fresh red chili, de-seeded and sliced very thinly in rounds

2 tbsp fresh Thai, or regular fresh basil leaves

1 tsp oil

2 - 6 oz red snapper filets

* can be found at Ellison's and Kootenay Co-op.

method

Combine tamarind and water in a small bowl and let stand for 10 minutes.

Rub tamarind with your fingers to dissolve it in the water.

Pour mixture through a sieve into a small saucepan, pressing firmly on solids to push through the sieve.

Discard remaining solid bits of tamarind left in sieve.

Add shallots, garlic, cilantro stems, fish sauce, sugar and salt to tamarind water and simmer for 2-3 minutes until thickened slightly.

Preheat broiler.

Brush fish with oil and season with salt and pepper.

Broil fish until just cooked through, about 7-8 minutes.

Add green onions, chilies and basil leaves into warm sauce and stir and heat for about 30 seconds until basil is wilted and chilies are warm.

Place fish on serving plates and ladle with the warm tamarind sauce.

Garnish with basil or cilantro leaves and serve with jasmine rice and steamed bok choy or your favourite greens.

Tamarind is made from the fruit that grows in large brown pods on the tamarind tree and gives a slightly sour flavor to Asian and Middle Eastern dishes. Keep it in the freezer and cut off a piece as needed.

butter chicken bowl

Referred to as "The Backside Bowl" at the Whitewater Ski Resort, this bowl of goodness makes a lot of skiers very happy! The food at our local mountain is absolutely amazing and this is a new lunch item offered by the talented Jeff Bruce, the Whitewater Kitchen Manager. Make this at home and serve it in your favourite big soup bowl.

Serves 8

ingredients

12 boneless and skinless chicken thighs

Rub

2 tbsp garam masala

1 tsp coriander

1 tsp harissa, paste or powder*

1 1/2 tsp salt

1/4 cup oil

Sauce

1 onion, diced

1 tbsp garlic, crushed and chopped

2 tsp ginger, peeled and grated

2 tsp coriander

1 tbsp salt

1 can (5.5 oz) tomato paste

1 tbsp oil

2 cans (400 ml) coconut milk

2 tbsp yellow curry paste

5 fresh tomatoes, diced

2 garlic cloves, crushed and chopped

1 1/2 tbsp ginger, peeled and grated

* found at Culinary Conspiracy

method

Mix together garam masala, coriander, harissa, salt and oil.

Rub the mixture all over chicken thighs and marinate for at least 4 hours.

Bake chicken thighs in 350°F oven for approximately 40 minutes and slice thinly or shred.

Sauté onion, 1 tbsp garlic, 2 tsp ginger, coriander, salt and tomato paste in oil for 5 minutes.

Add coconut milk and curry paste and let simmer for 30 minutes.

Add tomatoes, garlic, ginger and cooked chicken and simmer uncovered another 5 minutes to blend flavours.

At Whitewater Ski Resort, the Butter Chicken Bowl is served with basmati rice, fresh julienned spinach and topped with raita and a grilled piece of naan bread. Jeff has made this a dairy free version of "Butter Chicken" and the skiers are so excited!

quinoa crusted steelhead with tomato, leek and fennel compote

Steelhead is an ocean going trout and the colour is vibrant and the texture is like salmon. We love the idea of a crust topping on a fish and this protein filled topping is a healthy version with scrumptious results. The Tomato, Leek and Fennel Compote is fresh and light, completing this spa-like dinner!

Serves 4

ingredients

4 - 6 ounce pieces of steelhead

1/4 cup pine nuts, toasted

1 cup cooked quinoa

1 garlic clove, minced

1 lemon, zest of

1/4 cup olive oil

2 cups tightly packed green herbs (a mix of parsley, dill, mint, cilantro and basil) de-stemmed and chopped

1 tsp maldon salt (coarse sea salt)

1/2 tsp pepper

Tomato, Leek and Fennel Compote

2 tbsp extra virgin olive oil

2 cups leeks, sliced thinly

2 garlic cloves, minced

1 tsp fresh thyme, chopped

1 cup fresh fennel, sliced thinly

1/3 cup white wine

4 medium tomatoes, diced

1 tsp maldon salt

1/2 tsp pepper

1 tsp honey

1 tbsp fresh tarragon, chopped

method

Place pine nuts, quinoa, garlic, lemon zest, olive oil, salt, pepper and herbs in a food processer and blend until it forms a slightly chunky paste. Transfer to a small bowl and keep in fridge until ready to cook the fish.

Heat olive oil in medium saucepan over medium-low heat and add leeks, garlic, thyme, fennel and wine and cook until tender, about 10 minutes.

Add tomatoes, salt and pepper and continue to cook on medium-low heat for about 10 more minutes until tomatoes are just warm and still chunky, turn off heat and add the honey and tarragon.

Preheat oven to 400°F.

Place the steelhead filets on a baking sheet and rub with a bit of olive oil.

Spread the quinoa crust on each filet pressing with your fingers to make an even crust.

Bake the fish for about 15 minutes and serve on top of the warm Tomato, Leek and Fennel Compote.

The best and freshest fish in town is found at the Fisherman's Market, these guys know their fish!!

sides

miso gravy

You will LOVE the flavour and richness of this vegetarian and gluten-free gravy!! You will use it on EVERYTHING! From the Mushroom Nut Loaf in this book on page 96, to rice, yam fries, veggie burgers, grilled tofu and anything your palette desires. Shhh.... it's really good on chicken too!

Makes 4 Cups

ingredients

2 tbsp olive oil

1/2 onion, diced finely

1 tsp dried or fresh sage, chopped finely

1 tsp dried or fresh thyme leaves, chopped finely

1/2 tsp sea salt

1 tsp pepper

4 cups vegetable stock

2 tbsp tamari

2 tbsp balsamic vinegar

1 tsp lemon juice

1/2 tsp honey

1/2 cup nutritional yeast flakes

1/2 cup gluten free flour or regular flour

2 tbsp miso paste

1/2 cup parsley, chopped finely

method

Heat oil in a large, heavy bottomed pot on medium heat.

Saute onion until translucent.

Add sage, thyme, salt and pepper and sauté another 2 minutes.

Add 3 1/2 cups stock, tamari, balsamic vinegar, lemon juice and honey.

Stir well and then gradually add nutritional yeast, whisking constantly.

Combine flour and miso paste with the remaining 1/2 cup of stock and blend well until smooth in a small bowl.

Add to gravy, whisking very well to avoid lumps.

Simmer until gravy thickens, about 15 minutes.

Add parsley just before serving.

This gravy will keep for up to two weeks in the fridge – so make a double batch! As you reheat small portions, try adding a few sautéed mushrooms to make a nice miso mushroom gravy.

roasted brussels sprouts with crispy pancetta

Ahhh brussels sprouts – everyone will love brussels sprouts if you try this recipe. Roasting the little morsels with pancetta brings out a more vibrant flavour.

Serves 6-8

ingredients

1 tbsp olive oil

1/4 lb (115 g) pancetta, diced into 1/2 inch pieces

1/3 cup shallots, chopped finely

1/8 tsp red chili flakes

2 lbs brussels sprouts, trimmed and halved

1 lemon, juice and zest of

1/2 tsp salt

1/2 tsp pepper

1 tsp fresh thyme, chopped

method

Preheat oven to 350° F.

Heat olive oil in a large ovenproof sauté pan over medium heat.

Add pancetta and sauté for about 5 minutes until most of the fat is rendered and pancetta is nicely browned.

Add the shallots and the chili flakes and sauté until browned, about 3 minutes.

Add brussels sprouts, lemon juice and zest and toss everything together and let cook on medium high heat without stirring until slightly browned, 8-10 minutes.

Place pan in oven and roast for 15 – 20 minutes.

Remove from oven and season with salt, pepper and fresh thyme.

These also make a yummy and healthy appetizer. Serve warm and hand out the toothpicks!

rosemary, potato and artichoke tatin

This crispy potato tart is a savoury version of the classic French Tatin. Inspired by the amazing Yotam Ottolenghi, this delicious tatin can be served paired with a fresh green salad as a great summer lunch. Or you can move it to dinner as a beautiful side dish.

Serves 6

ingredients

1 1/2 cups cherry or grape tomatoes, halved

2 tbsp olive oil, divided

1 tsp salt

1 tsp pepper, freshly ground

1/2 lb nugget potatoes, skins on

1 large onion, sliced thinly

3 tbsp sugar

2 tsp butter

1 tbsp fresh oregano, chopped

1 tbsp fresh rosemary, chopped

1 cup artichoke hearts, drained and chopped coarsely

1 tsp sea salt

1 tsp pepper, freshly ground

1/2 cup (100 g) goat cheese, crumbled

1/2 package puff pastry, defrosted (Tenderflake)

method

Preheat oven to 300°F.

Place cut tomatoes, skin side down, on a parchment lined baking sheet.

Drizzle with 1 tbsp olive oil and sprinkle with salt and pepper.

Bake until dry for about 45 minutes.

Cook nugget potatoes in boiling, salted water until just done, about 15 minutes.

Drain and let cool.

Trim a bit off each potato end and discard, then cut in half.

Sauté onions in reserved 1 tbsp olive oil in a saucepan until golden brown, about 10 minutes, and set aside.

Brush a 9 inch round cake pan with oil or cooking spray and line the bottom with a circle of parchment paper.

Cook sugar and butter together over high heat in a small saucepan, stirring constantly with a wooden spoon to get a golden caramel.

Pour the caramel into the cake pan immediately and spread it evenly with the back of a spoon or by tilting the pan, over the entire bottom, it will harden a bit.

Scatter oregano leaves and rosemary over the caramel.

Arrange potato slices very closely together on the caramel lined bottom of pan.

Press tomatoes, then onions and artichoke hearts gently into the gaps and over top of the potatoes.

Sprinkle with salt and pepper.

Spread crumbled goat cheese evenly over vegetables and press down.

Roll out the puff pastry until it is about 1/8 inch thick.

Lay the pastry over the tart filling and trim with scissors or a knife to make a circle that is one inch bigger than the 9 inch pan.

Tuck the edges down around vegetables inside the pan.

Increase heat to 400°F.

Bake for 25 minutes, turn the oven down to 350°F and cook for another 10-15 minutes until pastry is golden brown.

Remove from oven and let stand for 2 minutes to let set a bit.

Hold inverted plate over top of baking pan and quickly flip both plate and pan together.

Lift off the baking pan.

Serve warm or at room temperature.

You can do the preparation for this tart in advance, keep it in the fridge and bake it the next day.

almond aioli

This vegan aioli is an alternative to conventional mayonnaise and is equally at home as a crudite or chip dip, or on your favourite sandwich.

Makes 1 cup

ingredients

1/2 cup blanched whole almonds

1/2 cup water

1/4 tsp garlic powder

3/4 tsp sea salt

1 cup sunflower or flaxseed oil

3 tbsp fresh lemon juice

1/2 tsp apple cider vinegar

method

Place almonds in food processor and grind to a fine powder.

Add 1/4 cup water, garlic powder and sea salt. Blend well, add remaining 1/4 cup water to form a smooth cream.

Drizzle oil into mixture with processor on lowest speed, blend until thick.

Add lemon juice and vinegar while processor is still running. Blend on low for another minute to allow mixture to thicken.

Transfer into glass jar with tight fitting lid and refrigerate for up to 2 weeks.

Even if you are not vegan, the almondy flavour of this aioli adds such a nice touch and the guilt of eating mayonnaise disappears!

celery root and potato gratin with caramelized onions

If you are tired of plain old mashed potatoes, try making this very rustic and classic French dish to accompany Sunday dinner.

Serves 6-8

ingredients

4 medium white onions, sliced thinly

1/4 cup maple syrup

1/4 cup brown sugar

1/4 cup balsamic vinegar

1 tsp salt

2 tbsp olive oil plus 1 tsp

1 head garlic, top part sliced off

2 heads celery root, about 1 1/2 pounds, peeled and chopped roughly

7 large Yukon Gold or russet potatoes, peeled and cut into chunks

3/4 cup milk or whipping cream or vegetable stock

3 tbsp butter

1 tbsp horseradish

1 tsp salt

1/2 tsp pepper, freshly ground

1 cup gruyère cheese, grated

3 tbsp fresh thyme, chopped

method

Preheat oven to 325°F.

Combine onions, maple syrup, brown sugar, balsamic vinegar, salt and 2 tbsp olive oil in a large bowl.

Spread the onion mixture onto a large shallow baking sheet and cover with foil.

Drizzle garlic with remaining 1 tsp olive oil and wrap in tin foil.

Put the onion mixture in the oven for two hours and the garlic for one hour.

Remove the onions from the oven and place in a bowl and squeeze the "flesh" of the roasted garlic in with the onions and combine.

Place the celery root and potatoes in a pot of salted water and cover.

Bring to a boil and then reduce the heat to medium and cook until very tender, about 25 minutes. Drain and return to pot and keep covered.

Preheat oven to 350°F.

Beat the potatoes and celery root until light and fluffy and then beat in the milk, (cream or vegetable stock) butter, horseradish, salt and pepper.

Spread the caramelized onion mixture in the bottom of an ovenproof baking dish.

Spoon the mashed potatoes and celery root over top of onions.

Top with grated gruyère cheese and chopped fresh thyme.

Bake until reheated and cheese is melted, about 40 minutes.

You can prepare this dish the day before and reheat it in the oven or microwave.

avocado hollandaise

This simple avocado cream is great on so many things! Poached eggs, salads, rice, quinoa, fish to name just a few.

Makes 1 cup

ingredients

1 ripe avocado

1 tbsp fresh lemon juice

2/3 cup hot water

4 tbsp extra virgin olive oil

1/2 tsp sea salt

1/2 tsp pepper

method

Place avocado, lemon juice and hot water in blender and puree until smooth.

Drizzle in olive oil, salt and pepper in the blender at low speed until just combined.

Store in a glass jar and keep in the fridge for up to a week.

My beautiful and amazing daughter Ali shared this with us. Thanks Ali!

gorgonzola and roasted walnut butter

This little gem is a perfect topping for a grilled steak or served with a crusy loaf of sourdough bread.

Makes 1 cup

ingredients

1/3 cup butter, room temperature

1/3 cup walnut pieces, roasted

1/3 cup gorgonzola cheese, crumbled

method

Place all ingredients in a small bowl and mash with a fork until combined.

Shape into a log, wrap in saran wrap and keep in freezer.

Slice off as needed.

Thanks Margie!

warm cherry tomato compote

This is a very simple yet so versatile condiment. After you make it once, you will be inspired to use it on everything. Fresh mozzarella, salads, omelettes, fish, pasta ...

Makes 1 1/2 Cups

ingredients

3 tbsp olive oil, divided

1 shallot, chopped finely

2 cups cherry or grape tomatoes, halved

1 tbsp red wine vinegar

1 tsp Maldon or any large flake sea salt *

1/2 tsp black pepper

2 tbsp fresh chives, chopped

2 tbsp fresh basil, chopped

method

Heat 1 tbsp of the olive oil in a medium sized saucepan over medium heat.

Add shallot and cook until soft, about 2 minutes.

Add tomatoes and cook, stirring occasionally, until juices begin to release, about 5 minutes.

Add vinegar and remaining 2 tbsp olive oil, salt and pepper.

Remove from heat and stir in chives and basil.

Serve warm or at room temperature.

Store in a glass jar, in the fridge for up to 2 weeks.

Maldon salt is a pyramid crystal sea salt from Great Britain and is available in specialty food shops and we love it!

gail's one pot grains

Do you love lots of different rice and grains in one dish but don't love all the pots involved in creating it? Gail is a chef at a cat skiing lodge and this is a recipe she swears by.

Serves 6

ingredients

1/4 cup olive oil

3 cloves garlic, crushed and chopped

1 red onion, diced

5 green onions, chopped

1/4 cup wild rice

4 cups low sodium chicken stock, divided

1/2 tsp dried oregano or 2 tsp fresh, chopped

1/2 cup pearl barley or quinoa

1/2 cup lentils, rinsed and drained

1/4 cup bulgur

1/2 cup pine nuts, toasted (or any other nuts!)

1/4 cup parsley, chopped

1 tsp sea salt

1 tsp pepper

1/4 cup parmesan, grated

method

Heat the oil over medium heat in a heavy bottomed stockpot.

Sauté garlic, red and green onions until soft, about 5 minutes.

Stir in wild rice, 2 cups of the chicken stock and oregano and bring to a boil.

Reduce heat, cover and simmer for 30 minutes.

Add the barley and another cup of the stock and simmer for 15 minutes.

Add the lentils and bulgur and remaining stock and bring to a boil again.

Reduce heat, cover and simmer until grains are tender, about 30 minutes.

Uncover and simmer until any remaining liquid evaporates.

Turn off heat and stir in the pine nuts, parsley, sea salt, pepper and parmesan.

This recipe makes a big batch but keeps well and reheats beautifully. You can serve it with a fresh filet of B.C. salmon and some beautiful asparagus or fiddleheads!

laura's mushroom and truffle risotto

The combination of mushrooms and truffles are like tomatoes and fresh basil, they are just meant for each other! This gorgeous recipe was shared by Laura Carter who is just one of those cooks who really knows her flavours. Her husband Reid is a very lucky guy!

Serves 4-6

ingredients

3/4 cup dried wild mushrooms, chopped roughly

1 cup chicken stock

1 mushroom bouillon cube

3 – 3 1/2 cups water

1/3 cup onion, diced

1 1/2 tsp butter

6-8 shiitake mushrooms, stems off and sliced

1 1/2 cups Arborio rice

1/2 cup Pecorino cheese, grated

salt to taste

3 tsp truffle oil

1/2 cup Pecorino cheese, shaved

method

Soak the dried mushrooms in 1 cup boiling water for at least two hours. Drain and reserve the liquid.

Combine the reserved liquid with the chicken stock, the mushroom bouillon cube and enough water to make 4 1/2 cups of stock in a large pot and heat to boiling.

Sauté the onion in butter until soft in a large frying pan or heavy bottomed stockpot on medium heat.

Add the sliced shiitake mushrooms and cook until they are soft.

Add the rice to the pan and cook until the grains become translucent with a white center.

Stir the hot stock, 1/2 cup at a time, into the rice and add more stock as it is absorbed into the rice until there is no stock left and turn off the heat.

Add the rehydrated mushrooms and grated Pecorino and stir in gently.

Add salt to taste.

Divide into pasta bowls, drizzle with truffle oil and top with the shaved Pecorino.

Serve this earthy and rich risotto with rack of lamb or steak or keep it light, paired with an arugula salad.

smiley creek sauce

After a fantastic mountain bike ride in Smiley Creek, Idaho, my amazing riding buddies and I came across this flavour packed sauce that was served on homemade veggie burgers in a tiny little road side café. We were famished after our big ride and this sauce on the veggie burgers made us so smug. This is for you Bonni!

Makes 1 1/2 Cups

ingredients

1/2 large red onion, cut into chunks

1 clove garlic, peeled and crushed

1/2 jalapeno pepper, seeded and chopped

2 cups cilantro, stems removed

1/2 tsp cayenne pepper

3 tbsp cumin

1 tsp sea salt

1/2 tsp pepper

1 lime, juice of

1/2 cup sour cream

1/2 cup plain yogurt

1 tsp maple syrup or honey

method

Place all ingredients, except sour cream, yogurt and maple syrup in a food processor and blend until smooth.

Add sour cream, yogurt and maple syrup or honey and pulse until smooth.

This sauce also adds a delicious zing to just about anything from grilled fish to appetizer platters. The veggie burger recipe from Whitewater Cooks pure simple, and real is the one we love.

jewelled rice

The exquisite Persian flavours in this stunning dish will tempt you to make it again and again. So embrace the lengthy ingredient list!

Serves 6

ingredients

1 cup water

1/2 cup sugar

2 medium carrots, peeled and julienned

1 orange, zest of

1 1/2 cups raw basmati rice

2 tbsp butter

2 tbsp olive oil

1 medium onion, diced

1 tsp salt

1/4 tsp cardamom

1/4 tsp cumin

1/4 tsp turmeric

1/2 tsp saffron threads, soaked in 1/2 cup hot water

1/4 cup dried cranberries, soaked in hot water for 10 minutes and drained

1/4 cup raisins, soaked in hot water for 10 minutes and drained

1/2 cup dried apricots, chopped and soaked in hot water for 10 minutes

1/4 cup unsalted pistachios, toasted

1/4 cup slivered almonds, toasted

method

Bring 1 cup water and sugar to a boil in a medium saucepan, stirring to dissolve sugar.

Add carrots and orange zest, reduce heat and simmer, stirring occasionally, about 15 minutes.

Drain saucepan with orange zest and carrots and discard the syrup.

Cook rice according to package instructions.

Heat butter and olive oil in a large frying pan over medium heat.

Add onion and salt and cook until soft, about 5 minutes.

Add cardamom, cumin, turmeric and saffron mixture and sauté for about 2 minutes.

Reduce heat to low and add cranberries, raisins, apricots, pistachios, almonds and the carrot and orange mixture.

Preheat oven to 325°F.

Grease an ovenproof casserole dish.

Put the cooked rice and the "jewel" mixture in the casserole and combine until well mixed.

Bake covered for 20 minutes.

Remove foil and garnish with more chopped pistachios.

Beautifully paired with any grilled meat or fish.

red onion confit

We use this on burgers, cheese boards and beef tenderloin crostini. It's always good to have a jar in your fridge!

Makes 2 Cups

ingredients

2 tbsp olive oil

3 large red onions, sliced thinly

2 bay leaves

2 tbsp fresh thyme, chopped finely

salt and pepper

1/2 cup brown sugar

3 tbsp balsamic vinegar

2/3 cup red wine

1 orange, zest of

method

Heat oil in frying pan on medium heat and add onions, bay leaves, thyme, salt and pepper.

Cook until onions are soft, about 10 minutes.

Add the brown sugar, balsamic vinegar, red wine and orange zest and cook on low heat until all liquid has reduced, stirring often – about 10 minutes.

Cool and store in a jar in the fridge for up to 2 weeks.

gussy's jack daniel's and mango barbeque sauce

Makes 3 Cups

Everyone needs a killer homemade barbeque sauce that can be brushed on all things grilled. This one has fresh mango, lots of garlic, orange zest and of course Jack Daniel's Bourbon and that says it all. Thanks to my incredible son Conner, for suggesting we include this.

ingredients

1/4 cup vegetable oil

1/4 cup red onion, diced

10 cloves garlic, crushed and chopped

1 tsp canned chipotle pepper, diced

1/4 tsp salt

1/2 tsp pepper

1 cup ketchup

1 1/2 cups diced fresh mango, or mango puree

1/2 cup apple cider vinegar

1/2 cup maple syrup

1/2 cup brown sugar

1/2 cup Jack Daniel's Bourbon

1 orange, juice and zest of

method

Sauté onion in vegetable oil until soft in heavy bottomed pot over medium heat.

Add garlic, chipotle pepper, salt, pepper, ketchup, mango, apple cider vinegar, maple syrup, brown sugar, Jack Daniel's and orange juice and zest.

Simmer on low heat for 15-20 minutes.

Purée until smooth with a handheld mixing wand if desired.

Serve Gussy's barbeque sauce on the side like a salsa.

desserts

tropical mountain loaf

Wrap these babies up in plastic wrap and stuff them in your cycling jersey or in your backpack for your next outdoor adventure. Super packed with fruit, seeds and berries, they are dense and delicious.

Makes 1 Loaf

ingredients

3/4 cup brown sugar

1/2 cup coconut oil, melted

3 bananas, ripe and mashed

1 egg

1/2 cup canned pumpkin

1/2 cup yogurt, plain

1 tsp vanilla

3/4 cup white flour

3/4 cup whole wheat flour

1 tsp baking powder

1 tsp baking soda

1/2 tsp salt

1/2 cup shredded coconut

1/2 cup pumpkin seeds

1/3 cup dried cranberries

1/3 cup dried blueberries

1/3 cup dried pineapple, chopped

method

Preheat oven to 350°F.

Grease one loaf pan.

Cream brown sugar and melted coconut oil in electric mixer.

Add bananas, egg, pumpkin, yogurt and vanilla and blend well.

Combine flours, baking powder, baking soda and salt in a separate bowl and mix well.

Add coconut, pumpkin seeds, cranberries, blueberries and pineapple to dry ingredients.

Fold dry ingredients into wet ingredients and combine by hand.

Spoon batter into loaf pan and bake for 1 hour or until skewer comes out clean.

Remove from oven and let cool in pan for 10 minutes, then transfer to cooling rack.

This recipe also makes 16 regular sized muffins, bake for 20 minutes.

red velvet beet cupcakes with raspberry icing

Red Velvet Cakes are all the rage and this one is super healthy, delicious and has vegan options.

Makes 12 large cupcakes or one 9" round layer cake

ingredients

Cupcakes

3/4 cup (398 ml) canned or fresh cooked peeled beets, pureed in food processor

1/2 cup vegetable oil

1/4 cup buttermilk or almond milk

3 tbsp sour cream or applesauce

1 tbsp balsamic vinegar

2 eggs (for vegan – 2 tbsp ground flax seed in 6 tbsp water)

3/4 cup flour or rice flour

2/3 cup sugar or cane sugar

1/2 cup cocoa powder, sifted

1 tsp baking powder

1/2 tsp baking soda

1/2 tsp salt

method

Preheat oven to 350°F.

Beat together beets, oil, buttermilk, sour cream, balsamic vinegar and eggs until well mixed.

Blend dry ingredients together in a separate bowl.

Add dry ingredients to wet and blend until well mixed, about 2-3 minutes.

Grease cupcake tin or line with baking cups.

Spoon batter into cupcake tin.

Bake for 15 – 20 minutes until skewer inserted comes out clean.

Ice when completely cooled.

Icing recipe continued on next page

ingredients

Cream Cheese Icing

1/2 cup butter, room temperature

1 cup cream cheese, room temperature

3 cups icing sugar, sifted

3 tbsp frozen raspberries, thawed and drained

Vegan Icing

1 cup frozen raspberries, thawed and drained

1/2 cup cashew pieces, soaked in 1 cup water for at least 30 minutes and drained

2 tbsp maple syrup

1/4 cup coconut oil, melted

method

Cream Cheese Icing

Place butter in food processor and blend until smooth.

Add cream cheese and process until butter and cream cheese are smooth.

Add icing sugar in two batches.

Add raspberries and process until smooth.

Spread on cupcakes.

Vegan Icing

Combine raspberries, cashews and maple syrup in food processor until smooth.

Add the melted coconut oil and blend again.

Pour into a shallow bowl and chill for a minimum of 2 hours.

Pipe or spread on cupcakes.

You can also make a lovely cake with this recipe. Pour batter into a 9 inch round cake pan and bake for 30-35 minutes.

chocolate hazelnut bark

This decadent little chocolate treat is a scrumptious mix of crunchy and creamy. Take a container on your next skiing, hiking or road trip and store the rest in the freezer!

Makes 3 Cups

ingredients

1 1/2 cups hazelnuts

1/4 cup butter, room temperature

1/3 cup brown sugar

1/2 cup flour, (gluten free flour is fine)

1/2 tsp sea salt

1/2 tsp cinnamon

8 oz milk or dark chocolate

1/3 cup hazelnut butter*

*Can be found at Ellisons Market and most specialty food stores.

method

Preheat oven to 350°F.

Place hazelnuts on a baking sheet and bake for 10-15 minutes or until golden brown.

When slightly cooled, rub the nuts with a clean tea towel until the brown skins fall off.

Separate the nuts from the skins, discard skins and place nuts in a bowl.

Reduce oven to 325°F.

Place 3/4 cup of the hazelnuts in a food processor and process until they are finely ground.

Set the other 3/4 cup of hazelnuts aside.

Cream butter and sugar until fluffy and light, about 5 minutes.

Add the ground hazelnuts, flour, salt and cinnamon and mix well.

Spread out on a parchment lined baking sheet.

Sprinkle the remaining hazelnuts onto the mix and bake for 15-20 minutes or until nuts are golden brown.

Cool to room temperature.

Melt the chocolate and hazelnut butter together in a large glass bowl over a pot of simmering water or in a double boiler.

Break up the cooled hazelnut bark into one inch pieces and add to melted chocolate.

Stir until bark is coated with chocolate and spread back onto a parchment lined baking sheet.

Cool in the freezer to harden. Break up into chunks and store in an airtight container.

Get creative and add dried cranberries, cherries or candied ginger. Put into your favourite Christmas tin for a yummy present.

sea salt and caramel nut squares

Sea salt and caramel is the newest, trendy flavour combo. Salt enhances sweet and maximizes the taste sensation of caramel, butter and nuts. A new twist on the original!

Makes one – 9 x 13 inch pan

ingredients

Crust

1 cup cold butter, cut into cubes

6 tbsp brown sugar

3 cups flour

1 egg

1 tsp fresh lemon juice

Filling

1 cup butter

2/3 cup honey

1 cup brown sugar

4 tbsp whipping cream

3 cups deluxe nut mix with macadamia and cashews, unsalted*

1 tbsp coarse sea salt

method

Preheat oven to 350°F.

Grease a 9 x 13 inch baking pan.

Place butter, sugar, flour, egg and lemon juice in a food processor and blend until mixture just holds together, but is still crumbly.

Press mixture into greased baking pan and bake for 15 minutes until golden brown and let cool.

Melt together butter, honey and brown sugar in a saucepan and let boil 7 – 8 minutes, stirring constantly.

Remove from heat and add whipping cream, whisking well.

Arrange nut mix on top of cooled crust.

Pour warm filling over nut mix, being careful not to move nuts.

Return pan to oven and bake for 20 minutes.

Remove from oven and sprinkle sea salt over the warm caramel.

Cool and cut into 12 pieces.

*can be found at Save- On- Foods

Any combination of nuts works well with these yummy squares.

blackberry hazelnut meringue with mascarpone cream

Crunchy and creamy at the same time. Hazelnuts and blackberries. Enough said!

Serves 8

ingredients

Meringue Base

1 cup hazelnuts, toasted and skinned

1/4 cup cornstarch

6 egg whites, room temperature

1 cup white sugar

Mascarpone Cream

1/2 cup mascarpone cheese, room temperature

1 tbsp fresh squeezed orange juice

1 cup whipping cream

1/4 cup icing sugar

2 tsp orange zest

3 cups fresh blackberries

method

Preheat oven to 350°F.

Process hazelnuts with cornstarch in a food processor until fine.

Beat egg whites in a clean dry bowl with an electric mixer, until soft peaks form.

Beat in sugar with mixer running, 2 tbsp at a time, until stiff peaks form.

Fold in hazelnut mixture gently with a whisk until evenly incorporated.

Form meringue into a round 9 inch circle on a parchment lined baking sheet using a spatula. Meringue will spread a bit while baking so ensure your baking pan is big enough.

Bake until dry and just firm to touch, for 45 to 50 minutes.

Remove from pan and let cool on rack for about an hour. Meringue can be made a few days in advance as long as kept dry and well wrapped.

Beat the mascarpone cheese and the orange juice with an electric mixer until smooth.

Add the whipping cream, icing sugar and orange zest.

Whip until the cream mixture forms soft peaks, about 1 minute. You can whip the cream just before serving or cover with plastic wrap and place in the fridge until ready to serve.

Assemble meringue just before serving.

Spread mascarpone cream on top of meringue base and scatter with 3 cups fresh blackberries on top.

Use any berries in season but we love the combination of blackberries with hazelnuts.

marsala poached blood oranges with creamy ricotta

An amazing dessert inpsired by the multi-talented Liz Abraham. This dessert is light, yet decadent and a flavourful, refreshing way to end dinner. Blood oranges are fantastic but you can use any combination of oranges that are in season.

Serves 8

ingredients

1 cup vanilla cane sugar

2/3 cup Marsala wine

2/3 cup water

1 lemon, juice of

1 orange, juice of

6 whole star anises

8 blood oranges

2 cups ricotta cheese

1 tsp sugar

1/2 tsp vanilla

method

Combine sugar, Marsala wine, water, lemon and orange juice and star anise in a saucepot. Bring to a boil, stirring occasionally and reduce heat to a simmer.

Peel skin of 5 of the oranges with a potato peeler. Strips should be 1/2 inch wide. Be sure to avoid cutting into the bitter white pith under the skin.

Stir strips into syrup and simmer until syrup is reduced by 1/3, stirring occasionally for about 20 -25 minutes.

Remove reduced syrup from heat and let cool.

Remove the remaining peel and white pith from all 8 oranges.

Slice each orange horizontally into 4 to 5 slices with a sharp knife.

Arrange orange slices in a pretty serving bowl.

Ladle the cooled syrup and candied peel over the oranges.

Chill until ready to serve, basting occasionally.

Whip ricotta cheese with the sugar and vanilla until well combined.

Serve in individual dessert bowls with a spoonful of whipped ricotta.

Luscious Olive Oil Cake on page 178 pairs beautifully with these oranges. If you would prefer not to use the ricotta, then try the Mascarpone Cream Recipe on page 166 for a rich and creamy alternative, or good old whipped cream.

berry uncheesecake

Our fun and adventurous friend Nancy Selwood shared this healthy recipe with us. When you have a hankering for cheesecake, but don't want all the calories, try this one. It has gluten-free options.

Serves 8-10

ingredients

Crust

1 cup large flake oats

1/2 cup whole wheat flour (substitute 1/2 cup sweet sorghum flour and 1 tsp xantham gum for wheat free)

1/2 cup finely ground almonds

1 tsp cinnamon

1/4 tsp salt

1 tsp vanilla

3 tbsp honey or maple syrup

1/4 cup vegetable oil

1 tbsp freshly squeezed orange juice

1 tsp orange zest

method

Crust

Preheat oven to 350°F.

Combine oats, flour, ground almonds, cinnamon and salt in large bowl and mix well.

Combine vanilla, honey or maple syrup, vegetable oil, orange juice and zest in a small bowl.

Add wet ingredients to dry ingredients. Be careful not to over mix.

Press firmly into bottom and sides of a 9 or 10 inch pie plate or a 9 inch fluted tart pan.

Bake for approximately 12 minutes until lightly browned.

Cool before filling.

recipe continued on next page

ingredients

Filling

1/2 cup millet

2 cups water

1/2 tsp salt

1/3 cup unsalted cashew pieces

1/3 cup freshly squeezed lemon juice

1 tsp grated lemon zest

1/3 cup maple syrup or honey

1 tsp vanilla

Topping

3-4 cups berries or sliced fruit (peaches, kiwis, nectarines)

3 tbsp fruit jelly or jam

method

Filling

Place millet in saucepan with water and salt and bring to a boil.

Simmer until water is absorbed and millet is soft, about 30 minutes.

Place cashew pieces, lemon juice, zest, maple syrup or honey and vanilla into a food processor.

Purée for about a minute until perfectly smooth.

Add warm millet to food processor mixture and pulse to combine, scraping down sides of bowl.

Process until creamy and smooth.

Pour into cooked pie shell, spread evenly and let cool and chill in fridge for 1 hour minimum.

Topping

Arrange fruit over filling.

Melt jam or jelly in microwave or small saucepan.

Brush melted jam or jelly over fruit with a pastry brush.

Chill for minimum of 1/2 hour before serving.

Don't tell anyone this "cheesecake" has no cheese, see if anyone notices!

jan's hornby island oat crackers

Traditional oatcakes are making a comeback and these are from the multi-talented Jan of Hornby Island who hopefully writes a gardening and cookbook herself someday and shares more of her secrets!! A savoury treat that is delicious with jam or a big hunk of sharp cheddar. Try these oat crackers with your afternoon tea.

Makes 3 Dozen

ingredients

2 cups large flake oats

1/2 cup flour

2 tbsp sugar

1 tbsp poppy seeds, or steel cut oats

1 tsp lemon zest

1/2 tsp baking soda

1/2 tsp salt

1/4 cup olive oil

1/2 cup hot water

method

Preheat oven to 350°F.

Mix oats, flour and sugar in food processor and pulse until well mixed and the oats are finely cut.

Add poppy seeds, or steel cut oats, lemon zest, baking soda and salt.

Mix olive oil and water together and add to food processor while it is running.

Pulse until dough just holds together.

Lay dough on a baking sheet lined with plastic wrap. Then place another piece of plastic wrap on top of dough.

Roll out to 1/8 inch thickness trying to keep a rectangular shape to fit pan.

Remove top sheet of plastic wrap and replace with parchment paper. Lay a second baking sheet on top of parchment paper and dough.

Hold baking sheets together and flip both over to get the dough onto the parchment lined baking sheet.

Remove plastic wrap from top of dough.

Cut dough with a knife on the baking sheet into cracker size pieces or cut out rounds using the top of a small glass.

Bake for 25-30 minutes or until slightly golden. Cool and store in an airtight container.

Add 1/2 cup of grated sharp cheddar to the dough right at the end of the food processor cycle for a cheesy addition.

sheri's sweet potato chocolate torte

There are many versions of this decadent chocolate slab of flavour, but this is our most favourite. Thanks Sheri!

Serves 12

ingredients

1 cup packed mashed sweet potato, peeled and cooked (cook them the night before if you like)

1 1/2 cups sugar, divided

1 cup almond flour

1/2 cup unsweetened dark cocoa powder, sifted

1/8 tsp salt

4 large eggs, room temperature

2 oz bittersweet chocolate

2 tbsp soy milk or whipping cream, room temperature

method

Preheat oven to 375°F.

Grease a 9 inch springform pan with butter or cooking spray.

Pulse sweet potato, 1 cup sugar, almond flour, cocoa powder and salt in food processor for 30 seconds or until smooth.

Separate 3 eggs. Set aside egg whites in a mixing bowl.

Add the 3 yolks and remaining whole egg to sweet potato mixture and pulse to combine.

Transfer sweet potato mixture to large mixing bowl.

Beat egg whites with electric mixer at high speed until soft peaks are formed.

Add remaining 1/2 cup sugar to the egg whites and beat 2 more minutes or until glossy peaks form.

Fold egg whites into sweet potato mixture in thirds with spatula.

Pour batter into prepared pan and bake for 45 minutes.

Cool for 10 minutes in the pan on wire rack before removing springform sides and then cool completely.

Melt chocolate in small bowl over simmering water and add soy milk or whipping cream and whisk to combine.

Spread over the top of the cake and smooth with a spatula.

Serve with Greek style vanilla yogurt or whipped cream and slightly frozen blueberries.

lime and pistachio loaf

A Middle Eastern take on traditional pound cake, we love the texture of this dense and buttery loaf. Drizzled with our favourite honey, Mellifera Bees, it is to die for!

Serves 10-12

ingredients

1 cup unsalted butter, room temperature

1 1/8 cups berry sugar (superfine sugar)

2 tbsp lime zest

1 1/2 tsp vanilla

6 eggs, room temperature

2 1/4 cups almonds, ground finely

1 1/2 cups pistachios, ground finely

method

Preheat oven to 325°F.

Line a lightly greased loaf pan with parchment paper.

Place butter, sugar, lime zest and vanilla in a mixing bowl.

Beat with an electric mixer for 10 - 12 minutes until pale and creamy, scraping down the sides of the bowl.

Add eggs, one at a time, beating well, after each addition scraping down sides of bowl.

Beat for a further 3 to 4 minutes until well combined.

Fold the ground almonds and pistachios into the butter and egg mixture until combined.

Place batter in loaf pan.

Smooth top with a spatula.

Bake for 60-70 minutes or until skewer inserted into middle of loaf comes out clean.

Cool completely in the pan at room temperature.

Remove loaf from pan.

Drizzle with your favourite honey to serve.

You can dress this loaf up or down. Cover with whipped cream and decorate with thinly sliced limes for a festive cake or serve plain with a nice cup of tea.

luscious olive oil cake

This is a very uncomplicated cake. The olive oil makes it so rich and moist and it pairs beautifully with the Marsala Oranges recipe on page 168. My Mom used to make one similar to this when we were young, I can picture it on our kitchen table decorated with fresh orange slices and dusted with icing sugar! This is a recipe shared by the "Queen of Cakes", Petra Lehmann.

Serves 8

ingredients

2 cups all purpose flour

1 3/4 cups sugar

1 1/2 tsp salt

1/2 tsp baking soda

1/2 tsp baking powder

1 1/3 cups extra virgin olive oil

1 1/4 cups whole milk

3 large eggs, room temperature

1 1/2 tbsp orange zest

1/4 cup fresh orange juice

1/4 cup Grand Marnier or sherry

method

Preheat oven to 350°F.

Prepare a 9 inch springform pan with cooking spray on sides and bottom and line the bottom with a circle of parchment paper.

Whisk the flour, sugar, salt, baking soda and baking powder together in a mixing bowl.

Whisk together the olive oil, milk, eggs, orange zest, orange juice and Grand Marnier in another bowl.

Add the dry ingredients to the wet until just combined.

Pour the batter into the prepared pan and bake for 1 hour, until the top is golden brown and skewer comes out clean when inserted.

Transfer the cake to a cooling rack and let cool for 30 minutes.

Run a knife around the edge of the pan, invert the cake onto the rack, remove pan and let cool completely for 2 hours.

Garnish with any type of edible flowers or kumquats and sliced oranges.

lemon curd tarte in a nut crust

This gorgeous tarte is reminiscent of patisseries all over France. The fresh citrus zing is a heavenly match with the crunchy nut crust.

Makes one 9 inch round or one 8 x 11 inch rectangular fluted tarte pan

ingredients

Lemon Curd

1 1/4 cup sugar

1 lemon, zest of

3/4 cup fresh lemon juice (about 2 1/2 lemons)

4 whole eggs, room temperature

4 egg yolks, room temperature

1 cup unsalted butter, room temperature, cut into 1 inch cubes

Nut Crust

1 1/3 cup flour

1/3 cup icing sugar, sifted

2/3 cup pecans, toasted and chopped finely in a food processor

1 lemon, zest of

1/4 tsp salt

2/3 cup butter, room temperature

method

Whisk together sugar, lemon zest, lemon juice and whole eggs and yolks in a medium mixing bowl until well blended.

Transfer into top of double boiler over simmering water and stir constantly until mixture thickens and coats the back of a wooden spoon, about 8 minutes.

Whisk in butter, one cube at a time, until completely incorporated.

Transfer to a glass bowl and let cool.

Combine flour, icing sugar, pecans, lemon zest and salt in a mixing bowl.

Cream butter in mixing bowl using electric beaters and then add dry ingredients until just incorporated.

Wrap dough in plastic wrap and let cool in fridge for 1 hour.

Press mixture into bottom and sides of a well greased fluted tart pan.

Return to the fridge for 30 minutes.

Preheat oven to 350°F.

Bake crust for 30 minutes and let cool. (If base of tart bubbles during baking, prick with a fork to allow steam to escape.)

Pour lemon curd into cooled crust and chill for at least 4 hours.

You can make the lemon curd a day ahead. Store it in the fridge overnight and bring to room temperature and whisk until smooth before filling the nut crust. Return the filled tarte to the fridge until ready to serve.

banana chocolate bread pudding with salted caramel sauce

Dense, super moist, maple soaked, but not too sweet – this dessert is an awesome way to use up over ripe bananas and stale bread. And the Salted Caramel Sauce is a deadly combination with the bananas and chocolate!

Serves 8-10

ingredients

5 large eggs, room temperature

5 egg yolks

2 1/2 cups whipping cream

2 1/2 cups half and half cream

1 tsp cinnamon

3/4 cup maple syrup

4 ripe bananas, mashed

1 tsp vanilla

6 cups French bread, torn or cubed into 1inch pieces

1 1/2 cups milk or dark chocolate, chopped into little chunks (Callebaut is best)

Salted Caramel Sauce

2 cups white sugar

1 tsp fresh lemon juice

2 tbsp water

2 cups whipping cream, room temperature

1 tsp maldon salt or any coarse sea salt

method

Grease large ovenproof baking pan with butter.

Beat eggs and egg yolks in a large bowl.

Add whipping cream and half and half cream and whisk together.

Whisk in cinnamon, maple syrup, mashed bananas and vanilla.

Add the cubed bread into the bowl, stir well and let bread soak up egg mixture for 15 minutes.

Preheat oven to 350°F.

Fold in chocolate chunks and pour into prepared pan.

Bake for 45 minutes or until bread mixture is firm to the touch.

Salted Caramel Sauce

Combine sugar, lemon juice and water in a heavy bottomed saucepan on high heat, bring to a boil and continue to boil without stirring until the sugar becomes a rich amber colour. You can swirl the pot around using the handles if needed.

Turn off heat and slowly whisk in the whipping cream, it will spit and spatter, so be careful.

Mix in sea salt and cool to room temperature.

Serve with the Bread Pudding.

The Salted Caramel Sauce can be stored in the fridge and reheated slightly before serving.

sander's mom's dutch spice cookies

Here is the right from scratch version of those yummy cookies that come in the bright red packages that you see in Holland. These ones are buttery and flavourful and actually come from a real Dutch Grandma!

Serves about 3 Dozen

ingredients

Spice Mix

4 tbsp ground cinnamon

4 tsp ground cloves

4 tsp ground nutmeg

2 tsp ground black pepper

2 tsp ground anise

3 cups white flour

1 1/2 cups brown sugar

5 tsp baking powder

2 1/2 tbsp spice mix

1 2/3 cups butter, cubed into 1 inch dice

1 egg

2 tbsp molasses

1/2 cup milk (optional)

1 cup slivered almonds (optional)

method

Combine all spice mix ingredients and set aside

Combine flour, brown sugar, baking powder and 2 1/2 tbsp of spice mix in large mixing bowl and blend well.

Cut butter into dry ingredients with a pastry cutter or two forks until pea sized and evenly mixed.

Blend egg and molasses in a separate cup with a fork or small whisk.

Pour egg mixture into dry ingredients and mix until combined.

Knead ingredients by hand until mixture forms a ball.

Cover and chill for one hour before rolling out.

Preheat oven to 300 °F.

Makes extra spice mix for your next batch of cookies.

Line two baking trays with parchment paper or grease them well.

Cut dough in half and roll out one half on each baking tray, leaving a 2 inch border around the entire edge of the tray.

Paint the entire cookie surface with milk and press slivered almonds lightly onto the top of the cookie. (This is optional).

Cut the rolled out dough into desired cookie size- about 2 x 3 inches.

Spread the individual cookies to the outside edges of the baking tray, spacing cookies evenly on the tray.

Bake for 25-30 minutes.

Score again on the cut lines and let cool.

emmy's kahlua ice cream cake

In Emmy's never ending repertoire of fabulous desserts, this one is in the top 10! If you've never made an ice cream cake, now is the time to try! The kids love this one!

Serves 10

ingredients

Cookie Crumb Layer

2 1/2 cups chocolate wafer cookie crumbs

1/2 cup butter, melted

3 tbsp sugar

Ice Cream Layer

2 litres good quality vanilla ice cream (Haagen Dazs or Breyers)

2 tbsp instant espresso powder

2 tbsp hot water

1 cup Kahlua or other coffee liqueur

Top Cake Layer

2 egg whites, room temperature

1 1/2 cups whipping cream

2 tbsp icing sugar, sifted

1 tbsp orange zest

1/4 cup Grand Marnier

Nanny Vance's Chocolate Sauce

1 cup sugar

1/2 cup cocoa powder

1/8 tsp salt

1/2 cup boiling water

1/4 cup butter

1 tsp vanilla

method

Cookie Crumb Layer

Preheat oven to 325 °F.

Combine cookie crumbs, melted butter and sugar in large bowl until well blended.

Grease a 10 inch springform pan.

Press mixture into bottom and sides of the springform pan.

Bake for 15 minutes.

Cool and set aside.

Ice Cream Layer

Place mixer beaters and bowl in freezer and chill for 30 minutes.

Dissolve espresso powder in hot water and cool in fridge.

Measure 1 cup of Kahlua and refrigerate.

Soften ice cream in fridge for about 30 minutes, until just "spoonable".

Place softened ice cream in frozen mixing bowl and beat with frozen beaters at slow speed.

Add cooled espresso mix and Kahlua gradually into ice cream.

Beat slowly, so as not to break the ice cream down, needs to be the consistency of soft ice cream.

Spoon into cookie crumb crust and freeze until solid, minimum 4 hours.

This cake can be made up to a week ahead.

Top Cake Layer

Beat egg whites until stiff and set aside.

Beat whipping cream until soft peaks form and then add icing sugar, orange zest and Grand Marnier.

Fold egg whites gently into whipped cream mix.

Spread this mix onto frozen ice cream layer in springform pan.

Freeze cake for one more hour.

Cut frozen cake with a hot knife and drizzle with Nanny Vance's Chocolate Sauce if desired.

Nanny Vance's Chocolate Sauce

Combine sugar, cocoa powder and salt.

Add boiling water and butter.

Bring to a rolling boil for one minute or to desired consistency.

Remove from heat and add 1 tsp vanilla.

little picnic cakes

These adorable and yummy little cakes are perfect for a picnic or potluck. No plates or forks, just a pretty basket or tin for packing and everyone can grab their own little treasure. We like to make several different toppings; fresh cherries and dark chocolate, pears and white chocolate, apricots and ginger, bananas and chocolate chips. The combinations are endless!

Serves 12

ingredients

3/4 cup flour

1/4 cup cornmeal

1 1/2 tsp baking powder

1/4 tsp salt

6 tbsp butter, room temperature

1/3 cup sugar

1 large egg

2 tsp lemon zest

1 tsp orange zest

1 tsp vanilla extract or almond extract

1/3 cup milk

1 1/2 cups fresh fruit of your choice

1/2 cup chocolate and/or nuts of your choice for topping

2 tbsp vanilla cane sugar

method

Preheat oven to 350° F.

Prepare a muffin tin with non-stick spray or cupcake liners.

Combine flour, cornmeal, baking powder and salt in a medium bowl and blend well.

Cream butter and sugar together in a bowl until light and fluffy – about 2 minutes.

Add egg, lemon and orange zest and vanilla. Beat until combined.

Add flour mixture and milk alternately in three additions, beating on low speed.

Divide the batter into the muffin cups. They will only be about 1/3 full.

Top with your chosen fruit, chocolate and nut combinations.

Sprinkle with sugar.

Bake until cakes are golden, about 20 – 25 minutes.

Let cool in the muffin tin, on wire rack.

These can easily be made a day ahead and stored in an airtight container. No need to refrigerate as the flavours will be better.

rosemary and sea salt brownies

The addition of sea salt to chocolate has become popular in the last few years. Then we added fresh rosemary to these wheat free brownies... ooh la la!!!!

Makes 1 – 8 x 8 inch pan

ingredients

1/2 tsp coarse sea salt, Maldon is best

1/2 tbsp fresh rosemary, chopped finely

2 tbsp extra virgin olive oil

5 oz good quality semi-sweet dark chocolate, chopped finely

1/2 cup butter, room temperature

1 cup brown sugar

1/2 cup ground almonds

1/4 cup rice flour

1/2 tsp baking powder

1/4 tsp xantham gum

1/2 cup dark cocoa powder, sifted

2 eggs, lightly beaten

1 tsp vanilla

1/2 cup chocolate chips or chunks (Callebaut is best)

method

Preheat oven to 350°F.

Grease an 8 x 8 inch baking pan and line with parchment paper.

Mix sea salt, rosemary and olive oil together in a small bowl with the back of a spoon (or with a mortar and pestle) and set aside for 10 minutes.

Melt the chocolate and butter in a double boiler, stirring gently.

Whisk together brown sugar, ground almonds, rice flour, baking powder, xantham gum and cocoa powder in a bowl.

You will love these unique brownies!

Combine the beaten eggs, vanilla, melted chocolate mix and rosemary infused olive oil together in a large bowl and beat on medium low for 2 minutes, until the batter thickens and becomes smooth and shiny.

Fold in the dry ingredients until just combined.

Spread into prepared pan.

Sprinkle with chocolate chips and press in slightly.

Bake for 30 minutes or until skewer comes out clean.

Cool and cut into desired size.

date and walnut cake with butterscotch cream

A fantastic wheat free cake that works really well for a special occasion. Make sure you buy the butterscotch schnapps because it is the bomb!

Serves 12

ingredients

Cake

3/4 cups fresh dates, pitted and chopped roughly

1/2 tsp baking soda

1/4 cup boiling water

1/4 cup butterscotch schnapps

6 eggs, separated, room temperature

3/4 cup brown sugar, divided

2 tbsp orange rind, grated finely

4 1/2 cups ground walnuts

method

Cake

Preheat oven to 325°F.

Line the base and sides of a lightly greased 9 inch springform pan with parchment paper.

Place dates, baking soda, boiling water and schnapps in a bowl and mash with a fork until just combined.

Transfer to a food processor and process until well combined.

Place the egg yolks, 1/4 cup brown sugar and orange rind in a large mixing bowl and beat with an electric mixer for 6-8 minutes, until thick and pale.

Fold the date mixture and the ground walnuts into the egg yolk mixture.

Place the egg whites in a clean bowl and using an electric mixer, whisk until stiff peaks form.

Add the remaining brown sugar to the egg whites gradually and whisk until stiff.

Fold the stiffened egg whites into the date and walnut mixture in 2 batches.

Pour into the pan and bake for 60-70 minutes or until a skewer inserted into the cake comes out clean.

Cool completely in the pan.

recipe continued on next page

ingredients

Filling

1 cup butter, room temperature

2 cups icing sugar, sifted

2 tbsp boiling water

2 tbsp butterscotch schnapps

1 tsp vanilla

Whipped Cream Topping

2 cups whipping cream

splash butterscotch schnapps

2 cups walnuts, toasted and chopped

method

Filling

Cream butter and icing sugar using an electric mixer until light and fluffy, about 2-3 minutes.

Add boiling water and beat well.

Beat in the schnapps and vanilla and whip for about 2 minutes until icing is light and creamy.

Invert cooled cake onto serving platter.

Cut the cake into three even layers and spread buttercream evenly between two of the layers.

Whipped Cream Topping

Beat whipping cream until almost thickened.

Add a good splash of butterscotch schnapps into the cream and whip until firm.

Cover cake evenly with whipped cream.

Press chopped walnuts onto the sides of the cake.

Chill until ready to serve.

All parts of this cake, except the whipped cream topping, can be prepared a day ahead. This makes for easy assembly and off your "to-do" list in the morning!

oatmeal chocolate avocado cookies

Have you decided to cut down on butter and wheat? Missing a yummy treat to have with your afternoon cup of coffee or chai tea? This cookie is a fantastic candidate to fill that gap! Made with rich avocado and chocolate chips, this cookie is deeply satisfying.

Makes 2 Dozen Cookies

ingredients

1 cup avocado, mashed

1/2 cup brown sugar

1/2 cup cane sugar

1 egg

1 tsp vanilla

1 cup gluten free flour

1/4 tsp xantham gum

1 tsp baking soda

1/2 tsp salt

1/2 cup medium sweet shredded coconut

2 cups quick oats

1/2 cup ground walnuts

1 cup chocolate chips (Callebaut are best)

method

Preheat oven to 325°F.

Place mashed avocado in large bowl and mix with electric beaters or a whisk until completely smooth.

Add both sugars and beat for another few minutes.

Add egg and beat until well incorporated.

Add vanilla and mix in.

Mix together in another bowl, the flour, xantham gum, baking soda and salt.

Add dry ingredients to wet and mix until well incorporated.

This is a fantastic gluten free recipe.

Add coconut, quick oats and ground walnuts and mix again.

Stir in chocolate chips.

Scoop out by large spoonful onto a parchment lined cookie sheet. Press dough down to flatten cookies to about 1/2 inch thickness.

Bake for 25 minutes or until cookies are lightly browned.

deconstructed apple baklava

A rustic version of traditional Greek baklava. This is going to become a favourite "go to" recipe, guaranteed! Thanks to the unflappable backcountry chef Marianne Abraham, for re-inventing this recipe that we loved from our movie catering days.

Serves 12

ingredients

1 package phyllo dough, frozen
3/4 cup butter, melted
1 cup pistachios, chopped finely
1 cup walnuts, toasted and chopped finely
1 cup whole almonds, toasted and chopped finely
1/2 cup sugar
2 tsp cinnamon
1/2 cup butter, melted
1/8 tsp salt
3 medium sized tart apples, peeled and chopped finely

Syrup
2/3 cup honey
4 tbsp butter
1 tbsp brown sugar
1/2 tsp cinnamon
1 tsp lemon juice
1 orange, juice and zest of
2 tsp vanilla

method

Preheat oven to 350°F.
Grease a 9 x 13 inch baking pan.
Remove outer plastic wrap from phyllo and let thaw on counter until you can unroll it.
Unroll and remove inner plastic separator sheet. Reroll phyllo.
Cut phyllo roll into 3/4 inch pieces.
Transfer phyllo pieces to large bowl, tossing with the melted butter until well coated and ribbon like.
Place half of the phyllo ribbons into the baking pan. Press firmly until it is fairly compact.
Mix chopped nuts, sugar, cinnamon, melted butter, salt and chopped apples and spread over base layer.

Cover loosely with the other half of the phyllo ribbons.
Bake for 25 minutes until phyllo is golden brown. Make the syrup while the baklava is baking.
Mix together all syrup ingredients in a saucepan and bring to a low boil.
Whisk constantly while on a low boil for 10 minutes.
Remove from oven and immediately pour hot syrup over hot baklava.
Serve slightly warm with your favourite vanilla ice cream.

Also a great way to use up that phyllo dough in your freezer that is no longer in perfect shape.

index

dinners

sides

desserts

for ali, conner and mike